The BED BOOK

An Original Harvest/HBJ Book

Mark Dittrick

The BED BOOK

Harcourt Brace Jovanovich/New York and London

Printed in the United States of America

Library of Congress Cataloging in Publication Data

Dittrick, Mark.
The bed book.

(An Original Harvest/HBJ book)
1. Beds and bedsteads—History. 2. Beds and bedsteads. I. Title.
GT450.D57 392'.36 79-1856
ISBN 0-15-611322-8

First Original Harvest/HBJ edition

A B C D E F G H I J

CONTENTS

The BED BOOK

Patented Nov. 17, 1925. 1,561,979

UNITED STATES PATENT OFFICE.

ROBERT HAYES GORE, OF CHICAGO, ILLINOIS.

EXERCISE BED.

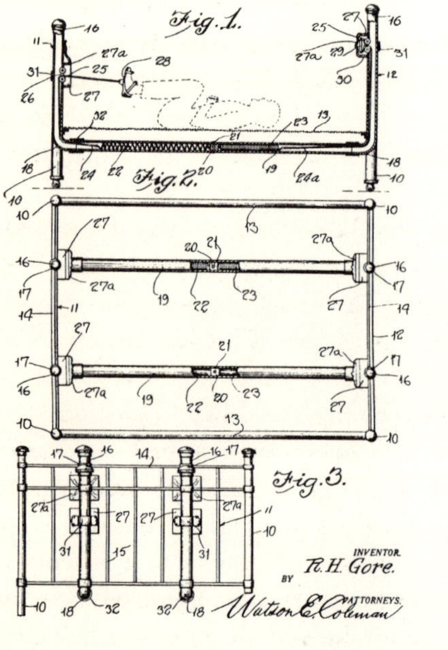

To all whom it may concern:

Be it known that I, Robert H. Gore, a citizen of the United States, residing at Chicago, in the county of Cook and State of Illinois, have invented certain new and useful Improvements in Exercise Beds, of which the following is a specification, reference being had to the accompanying drawings.

This invention relates to beds, and particularly to metallic beds, and the general object of the invention is to provide a bed so constructed that exercises may be taken therein while lying upon the bed.

A further object is to provide a bed of this character having coiled contractile springs arranged in the bottom of the bed, pulleys arranged in certain posts of the head board and foot of the bed, and flexible cords attached to the springs and extending over said pulleys and by which the arms and legs of the person lying in the bed may be readily exercised.

A still further object is to provide a device of this character having posts forming part of the head and foot board of the bed, the cords being conducted through said posts and out of openings therein, one pair of cords being provided with means whereby the feet may be connected to the cords and the other being provided with handles, these tubular posts being provided with housings whereby the handles and foot-connecting parts are housed and concealed.

My invention is illustrated in the accompanying drawing, wherein:—

Figure 1 is a vertical sectional view of an exercising bed constructed in accordance with my invention, showing in dotted lines the method of using the bed;

Figure 2 is a top plan view of the structure shown in Figure 1;

Figure 3 is an end view looking toward the foot board.

INTRODUCTION

"The bed, my friend, is our whole life. It is there that we are born, it is there that we love, it is there that we die."

Le Lit, by Guy de Maupassant

The great 19th-century French novelist forgot to mention that most of us were also conceived in a bed. Someone who was conceived on a grassy field or someone who was born on the way to the delivery room in the back of a Buick might still be left unimpressed. Yet they might do well to consider some perhaps more relevant reflections on the importance of the bed.

"After all, you spend a third of your life in bed . . . why not in a great bed?" asks a line from a custom mattress manufacturer's brochure. "Most of us spend a third of our lives in bed. Reason enough for us not to dismiss the bed itself lightly," begins a magazine article on how to shop for a bed. "So, you've finally decided to replace that twenty-year-old mattress and you're not sure where to begin. You'd like to pick one up for nothing, but you realize a third of your life is spent in bed . . ." runs the lead-in headline atop a furniture store newspaper advertisement. Approximately a third of each day, if you missed the point all three times, is spent in bed. That would add up to more than 1,100 weeks in a seventy-year lifetime. Over 8,000 days. 195,000-plus hours. You can figure out how many minutes and seconds. We may not be awake and aware of our being there all the while that we're there, but we're there that long just the same.

Ask yourself this: What will be the very last thing you do today? Go to bed. And the very first thing tomorrow, before doing anything else (in fact, in order to be able to do anything else)? Right again. You'll get out of a bed.

If you had to give up every stick of furniture save one, which one would you choose to keep? A chest of drawers? A coffee table? A secretaire? A chiffonier? An etagere? Or maybe a chair?

The bed is the most used of furniture pieces. Chairs and tables are often used purely for ornament, something that seldom, if ever, happens to a bed. And what other item of furniture has a room named after it?

If only our imperfect bodies had more natural cushioning to protect our poorly padded bones against the hurts of a hard horizontal surface; then the bed might be less of a necessity. But necessary it is, as needed by hard-boned humans the world over as sleep itself. So, as the twilight edge of the great shadow of night gobbles up long lines of longitude on its inexorable east-to-west march around the globe, the weary humans in its path respond to its coming in the same predictable way—the Fijian retiring to an *i mocemoce*; the Eskimo bundling up and settling down on an *iglerk*; Zulus turning in on an *umbhede wesingili*; the Albanian stretching out on a *shtrat*, the Lithuanian on a *lóva*, the Indonesian on a *tempat tidur*, and those who inhabit the English-speaking world on a bed.

It seems fitting to end these few thoughts, which began with a quote from a most quotable Frenchman, with a note about a most notable Frenchman who was equally aware of the importance of the bed—Napoleon Bonaparte's nephew Louis Napoleon, who in 1852 (when de Maupassant was only two years old) became France's second emperor and changed his name to Napoleon III. Times were lean when Napoleon III assumed power; the government maintained a national pawnbroker's office (called the Mon-de-piete) where insolvent citizens could trade in their meager possessions for a much-needed sou or two, and the new emperor decided that the very best way to endear himself to his new subjects would be to declare out-of-hock something they would appreciate getting back. Thousands of mattresses, he learned, had been pawned; so Napoleon's first grand, beneficent gesture to the people of France was to give them back their beds.

A QUICK HISTORY OF THE BED

Tommy Dale Palmore's I Think We're Alone Now, *acrylic on canvas, Pennsylvania Academy of the Fine Arts, Philadelphia.*

Roughly 32,000 years ago, the last great ice sheet retreated to the north where it belonged, leaving behind it the tool-wielding *Homo sapiens* who were destined to dominate the defrosted landscape. What these early Neolithics used for beds is a guessing game. Presumably, they did at some point begin doing something to soften the spots where they slept and employing some form of covering to keep off the cold. Animal skins probably served to do both.

The earliest known beds may have been constructed by the ancient Egyptians, whose very civilized civilization sprang up on the banks of the Nile around 3200 B.C. Some benevolent god must have declared "Let there be furniture," for the craftsmanship seen in Egyptian beds that have sur-

The beds of our ancient ancestors were often surprisingly sophisticated, and apparently fairly comfortable. An example is this one from Egypt's XI Dynasty (2134–c. 2000 B.C.). Beneath linen sheets and a "mattress" of folded fabric is a wooden frame lashed to short legs ending in hoof-on-paw feet. A wooden headrest completes the bed; a box containing toiletries sits next to it.

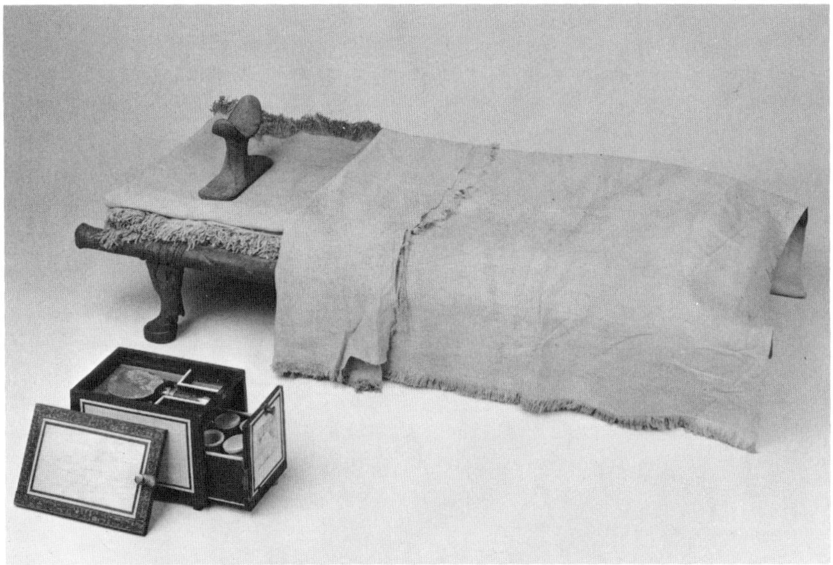

This reproduction of a wall painting found in the tomb of Tutmose III, ruler of Egypt c. 1450 B.C., shows artisans busily turning out artifacts. The two craftsmen pictured in the lower right-hand corner are working on a bed with lionesque legs (ending in lion paws-on-pads) and a lion's head. They are shown boring holes in the bed's frame through which cords that lash a woven mat to the frame are threaded.

A two-piece ivory headrest found in the tomb of the Egyptian boy king Tutankhamen (c. 1350 B.C.). The kneeling figure shouldering the head support and flanked by protecting lions is the god Shu.

vived, especially those from later periods, is truly astonishing, by both ancient and modern standards.

The very earliest Egyptian beds were relatively simple: rectangular frames of thick palm ribs or cedarwood, set on and lashed to short legs of the same material with leather thongs or fibrous cords. Filling the long horizontal opening in the frame was a woven mat of flax that was tied to the frame's sides. This world's first mattress foundation created a resilient and comfortable surface for sleeping. To make it even more inviting, layers of cloth, animal skins, and even stuffed cushions were placed on top. Linen sheets were also quite common.

But there were no pillows. Egyptian heads were supported, as heads are to this day in many parts of the world, by hard, stoollike headrests. Headrests were generally carved out of wood, but ivory was also frequently used. A particularly beautiful headrest carved from a solid block

Furniture that folded up for storage or transport was an ancient Egyptian innovation. This example, a multihinged camp bedstead, was found in the tomb of Tutankhamen.

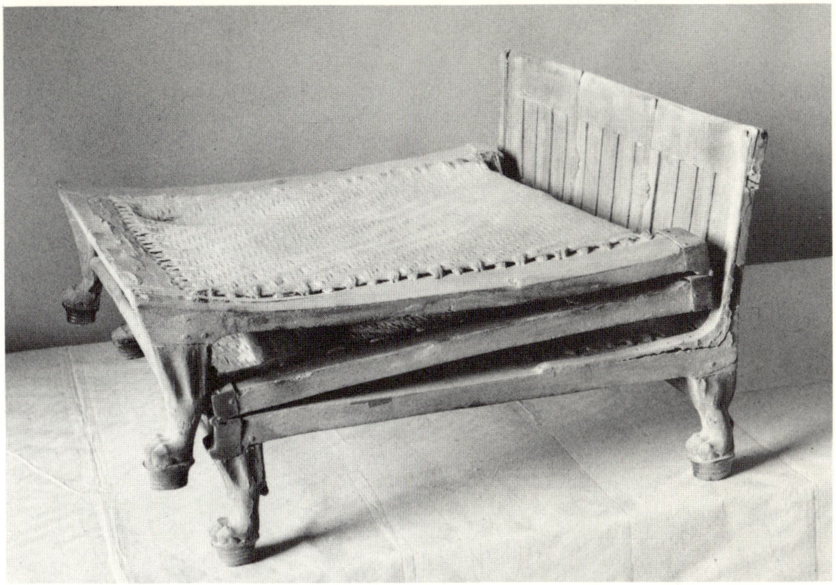

of glass was found in the well-known tomb of Tutankhamen, along with a sizable collection of beds.

By Tut's time (c. 1350 B.C.), Egyptian beds were grand. Some were sheathed in gold; others were fabricated entirely of ivory. Mortise-and-tenon joinery was used to hold the parts together. Collapsible beds (some bearing a disturbingly close resemblance to modern aluminum and plastic-webbed lawn chairs) that folded up on bronze hinges were common. The legs of beds, which had once been simple in shape, turned into the legs of animals, those of the lion being by far the most popular. And there was a footboard rising up above the horizontal plane of the bed, from the end opposite the headrest.

Some Egyptian beds had canopies from which a kind of mosquito netting was hung. Beds and canopy frames from the later periods could be dismantled and easily transported about. If nothing else were available to today's Western sleeper, the beds the ancient Egyptians slept on would serve perfectly well; the headrest, though, might take some getting used to.

The peoples who closely followed the Egyptians into the civilized world—the Mesopotamians, Babylonians, Assyrians, Phoenicians, and some others—all slept on beds that were remarkably similar, and not too unlike the ones slept on by the Egyptians. The frames were heavier and less refined, they tended to rise higher off the ground, and they were somewhat more couchlike than the beds of Egypt. And those that the top of the heap climbed into were quite large and obviously designed to impress. Ivory, ornately carved, was a favorite material. But the people east and north of Egypt did make one significant contribution to the development of the bed: the footboard left the foot of the bed and relocated at the head, becoming a headboard, an innovation that is obviously still with us today. The headboard's reason for being, it seems, was to provide a place for piling cushions, a practice that did away with the headrest. Beds such as these also served as couches during the day.

This was true, too, of the couch-cum-bed of the ancient Greeks, who had a name for it: *kline*. Their beds went back to a simpler form, with a lighter, more Egyptian-like frame. The legs usually were carved to look like an animal's; when they weren't, they were usually turned on a lathe (especially after 700 B.C.), a new twist for bed supports.

Thongs threaded through holes in the frame and back and forth across the opening provided a springy support for the mattress, which was stuffed with anything from straw to swansdown. Linen sheets and purple-dyed woven blankets or the fleeces of sheep were used to cover the sleeper.

Odysseus, during his Odyssey, made a bed from a solid piece of olive wood. He then decorated it with inlays of ivory, silver, and gold. The indulgent inhabitants of Sybaris, a Greek city in Italy founded around 720 B.C., are said to have slept on beds of roses. (The city was sacked around 510 B.C., and life for the self-pampering Sybarites was presumably no bed of you-know-what from that date on. Nor was it for poor Greeks in general, some of whom, it has been written, generally slept on the

From the 1st-century A.D. Roman resort city of Herculaneum, sister city to Pompeii, came this beautiful symmetrical ivory couch/bed with its decorations of carved bone and glass inlay.

A 6th-century B.C. pinax, or plate, from Corinth, showing a poet (note the lyre) stretched out on a Greek bed typical of the period. Sleepers used footstools to climb up to a sleeping surface lifted off the ground by tall turned legs.

ground on the untreated skin of a bull, with one half of it under them and the other half over.)

The Romans, who began building their empire during the first millennium B.C., had couchlike beds in a wide range of sizes. A single bed was called a *lectuli*. A bed for two was a *lecti geniales*. There was even one, called a *triclinia*, that had room on it for three. And they ranged from simple to fancy, depending, of course, on the means of the sleeper. The lowliest of the lowly slept on a *grabatus*, a crude arrangement of roughly hewn wood set low and close to the bug-infested ground, or on a simple stone shelf built out from a wall. Those citizens who were better off reclined on wooden couches of the Greek kind, while an affluent Roman might have a bed cast in bronze, or a fancy wooden one richly inlaid with tortoiseshell, or with legs of carved ivory. Heliogabulus, who was the emperor for a very short time (from 218 to 222 A.D., the year in which he was assassinated), was also the leader of a cult of sun worshipers; he slept on a solid silver bed.

On a webbing that was stretched across the frame of the Roman bed the mattress (*torus*) was placed, and a stuffed, bolsterlike cushion (*culcita*) was used as a pillow. There was, however, no need for sheets or blankets, for Romans, both women and men, left on most of their clothes when they retired. Or they took off only the toga to use it as a blanket.

Beds were placed in a special bedchamber called a *cubiculum*, a closetlike, stuffy little room with tiny windows that let in almost none of the morning light. The bed was normally the only article of furniture inside. It was no wonder that the average Roman who awoke in such uninspiring surroundings wasted little time in starting his day: "The emperor Vespasian used to drape himself unaided in half a minute, and the moment he had put on his *calcei* he was ready to give audience and set about the performance of his imperial duties. The Romans of this period were thus ready to the business of their public life within a few minutes of getting out of bed. Their breakfast consisted of a glass of water swallowed in all haste. They did not waste time in washing for they knew they would be going to the bath at the end of the afternoon," writes Jerômé Carcopino in his *Daily Life in Ancient Rome*.

When B.C. turned A.D., Augustus was emperor in Rome, and in Pompeii to the south people were sleeping on beds that were set into alcovelike

An anonymous painting on silk from the Sung Dynasty (960–1279) in China shows a simple bamboo bed of the period and its occupant, comfortably sleeping with his head propped up on a long, square pillow.

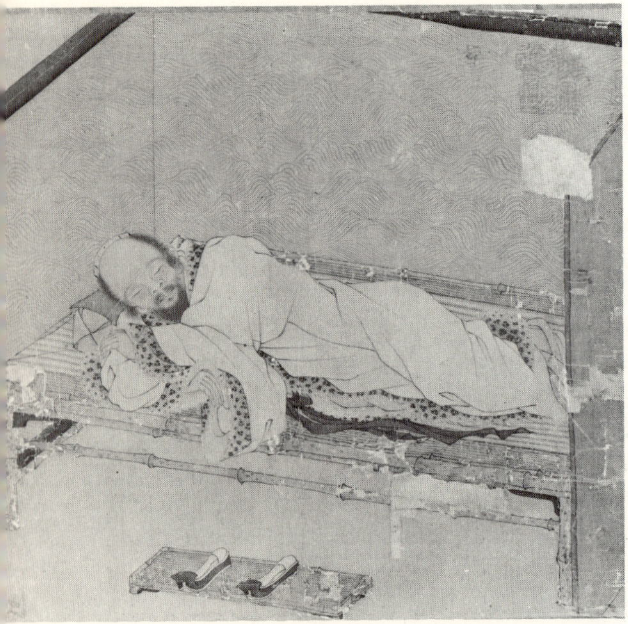

niches built into the walls of their houses. In 79 A.D. Vesuvius erupted and buried in ashes Pompeii and the Pompeiians, some still on their beds in their niches, until the city was discovered in 1748, preserved in nearly perfect condition after almost 1,600 years.

But about 400 years after Pompeii went undercover, the Romans found themselves up to their eyeballs in Goths, who eventually destroyed the city and every stick of furniture in sight. The cloud of the Dark Ages fell over the once classical landscape, and the classical bed in Europe was dead.

After Rome's fall the people of Europe, both the rich and the poor, found themselves surrounded by sleeping arrangements that harked back to the days before the dynasties of Egypt. For the poor it wasn't a dramatic change: they had been sleeping pre-Egyptian all along. And the people up north, in the land of the Goths, didn't know any better way to sleep than in the way that prevailed throughout the continent: on a pile of straw on the ground, or on the ground on a sack filled with straw, or on straw that filled a troughlike bench, or on a straw mattress laid across the top of a chest. That was the extent of the options. Between the 5th century and the year 1000, a physical piece of bedlike furniture was next to nonexistent.

But the classic skills hadn't been entirely lost; they were alive in the East, in Constantinople, the new center of the Christian world. There, East was meeting West, and the beds were made a little bit Roman and a little bit Greek. And turnery—shaping wood and similar materials on a lathe—was a much-practiced technique used for turning out those hybrid beds' legs. Many of the skills being maintained returned in a few hundred years to the medieval world, where in the meantime furniture was slowly being reinvented.

By the 11th century, bedsteads—at first nothing more elaborate than shallow rectangular boxes on plain, stubby legs—began to appear. Soon they had nicely turned legs and some tentative touches of ornamentation. But the end of the century was to witness an event that would have a profound effect on the look of beds for hundreds of years to come. Pope Urban II exhorted the armies of Europe, in 1095, to take up their swords and reclaim the Holy Lands from the Muslims. They went off on the First Crusade, and they brought back curtains.

Very easy on the eyes but seemingly less so on the head is this enameled pottery pillow from the time of the T'ang Dynasty (618–906 A.D.) in China.

By the 12th century, every decent bed was surrounded by curtains. They were hung from the ceiling or attached to hooks in the walls, drawn open in the daytime and pulled shut at night. The fabrics they were made from grew richer and richer, and the amount of space they enclosed increased in size. Beds, which had always been situated in the single main hall, now functioned as self-contained rooms. And something else Urban II hadn't counted on happened now that curtains could keep out the cold: people started stripping themselves completely naked at night.

Had the wooden part of the bed not been totally covered by drapes, it might have developed in style. But since it was little more than a frame for curtains, it stayed remarkably crude for a long time. It wasn't even considered a legitimate part of the bed, simply the object around and on which the hangings and crude feather- or straw-stuffed mattress, the real "bed," went.

And the beds of the nobles went quite often, from castle to castle to castle. Staying too long at one lordly address during those troubled times wasn't considered a safe thing to do. So the nobility had mobility and so did their beds, which they dropped on top of whatever empty frame was available.

Farther north, where nobles traveled less frequently, curtains were sometimes replaced by wood paneling, and beds became rooms within rooms. This innovation—the box bed—persisted almost to the 20th century and even found its way to the New World.

Wooden furniture, of which there was still very little, started conforming to recognizable styles. Beginning in France in the 12th century, and spreading to many parts of Europe, especially the north, over the next four centuries, was a style we now call Gothic. Heavy, solid oak furniture was elaborately carved with motifs that copied the pointed arches and rosettes that adorned contemporary cathedrals. In the southern part of the continent, the favored style was Romanesque. The basic shape of the furniture was the same, but the carving, as the name suggests, was reminiscent of old Rome. Both new looks turned up on beds.

The 14th century brought another bed innovation: the tester, a framework that was attached to or slung from the ceiling, or jutted out from the wall, and from which curtains were hung. But all progress in beds, and in everything else, came to a sudden halt by something else the

14th century had brought: the Black Death. When the great plague of 1349, which took away over a third of Europe's population, finally lifted, it left an enormous surplus of everything—land, cattle, houses, and furniture, including some of the very finest 14th-century beds. The poor suddenly found themselves unexpectedly rich and sleeping on mattresses of down. A devastating inflation then followed (such is the life of the poor), and the riffraff was soon back to sleeping on straw.

While much of 15th-century Europe was just starting to stir from its long medieval sleep, in Italy the Renaissance was beginning to bloom. Italian beds came out from behind their curtains and showed newly bared posts (and legs and some other parts now exposed) that were energetically carved, and sometimes also gessoed and painted or gilded, but with classical restraint. In other parts of Europe the beds remained covered, but there were other developments in the making.

Testers were being carried by the posts of the bed. In Germany and other northern countries, beds blended into the corners of rooms, built right into them and covered with paneling that matched the walls.

The noble had settled down by now, but his phobias mothered a new bed invention. Houses had more rooms than ever before, and the nervous noble had his own separate bedchamber. Feeling in danger sleeping alone, he (or she) had a guard (or a guardess) sleep close by in the room. The protector slept on a low bed with wheels that rolled out from under the protectee's bed at night, and back under and out of the way during the day. It was called a truckle, and sometimes a trundle.

Was this the world's first platform bed? Perhaps. The large platform on which this late-15th-century Italian Renaissance walnut bed rests provided plenty of seating for visitors and lots of storage space for bedding.

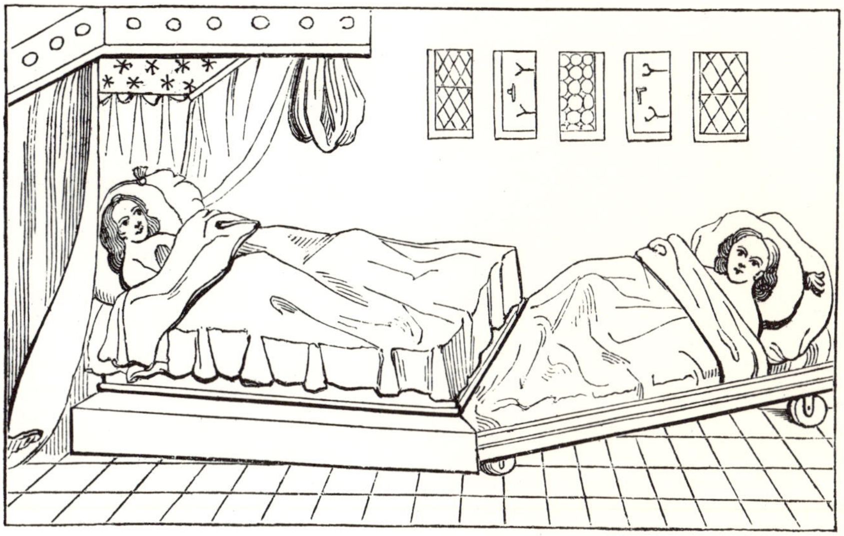

A medieval illustration of an early form of the trundle, or truckle, bed.

Lits de camp (also called trussed beds) that collapsed and folded up were, at first, used for strictly military occasions. They grew increasingly fancy, though, supported bright colorful curtains, and gained great favor with the ladies.

Kings of France began reclining on a *lit de justice*, from which they carried out the formal business of the state. And nobles followed the example on their *lits de parade*, grand beds on which one received important guests.

Beds all over France started showing their wood as the Renaissance influence spread. Sixteenth-century Frenchmen and ladies slept on *lits de colonnes*, which had elaborately carved posts supporting testers. At the same time in England, similar Tudor beds—blends of Gothic and Renaissance—grew to incredible sizes. The famous Great Bed of Ware, made around 1575, measures approximately eleven feet long by a little more than eleven feet wide.

The part of the bed where the mattress went was still just a big shallow box. It was usually filled with straw, covered by a large canvas sheet, and a featherbed rested on top. Henry VIII had his royal straw ceremoniously changed every day.

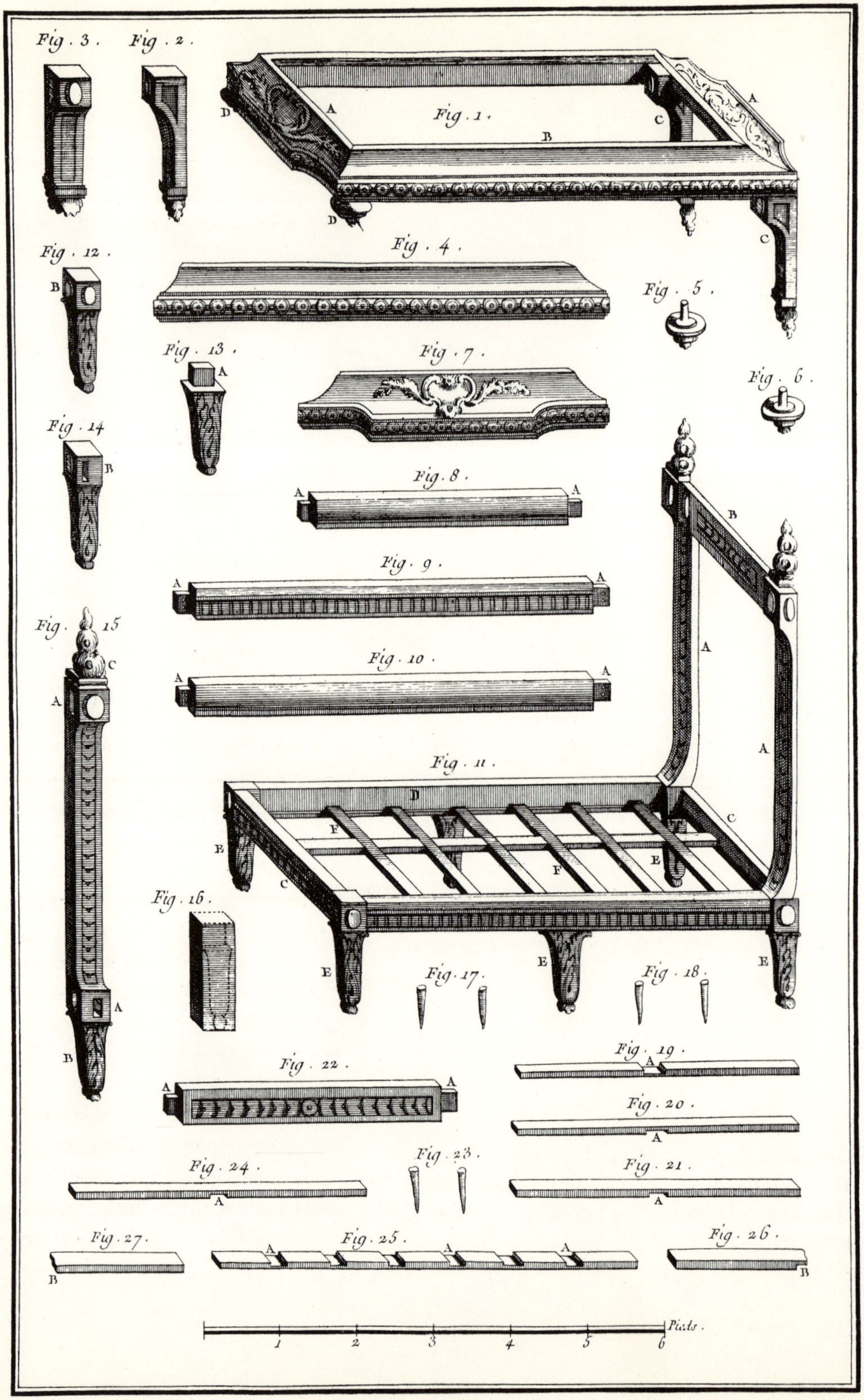

Fig. 3.
Fig. 2.
Fig. 1.
Fig. 4.
Fig. 5.
Fig. 6.
Fig. 7.
Fig. 8.
Fig. 9.
Fig. 10.
Fig. 11.
Fig. 12.
Fig. 13.
Fig. 14
Fig. 15
Fig. 16.
Fig. 17.
Fig. 18.
Fig. 19.
Fig. 20.
Fig. 21.
Fig. 22.
Fig. 23.
Fig. 24.
Fig. 25.
Fig. 26.
Fig. 27.
1
2
3
4
5
6
Pieds.

The 17th century found bedmakers going for Baroque, inventing a new monumental and masculine style. And curtains returned in a big way. More impressive and lavish than ever, they once again completely overwhelmed the frame, which itself was climbing to new heights. *Vaillains* were drapes that adorned the bed's topmost parts. *Basses* hid the space underneath. The heavy side curtains were called *bonegraces.* Rich embroidery covered nearly everything; braids and fringes and tassels dangled all around. The posts that supported the drapes were often surmounted by plumed *panaches.*

The *lit de repos*, or daybed, an elongated seat with a raised, pillowlike end, was another major development, and Louis XIV, the *Roi-Soleil*, had forty-eight of them at Versailles.

The *lit en housse* had a new kind of tester, up and into which the curtains were raised like a blind.

The poor, however, still slept poorly. The servants in some of the great houses slept on pallets placed on the floor at night and rolled up in the morning. In Ireland's rural countryside people lived in huts made of mud, with no windows or chimneys, and slept on the floor with their animals.

The 17th was the century that marked the beginning of serious colonization in the New World. The Dutch who settled New Amsterdam brought their featherbeds with them, along with brass warming pans. The Pilgrims of Plymouth spent their famous first winter on beds (presumably lacking brass warmers) of the simple lowpost variety, a plain turning on a post here or there the only decoration the Puritan life-style would allow.

The early French settlers in Canada slept in large cabinetlike boxes called *cabanes.* Similar to, but more rustic than, the enclosed beds (*lits clos*) of Brittany and Auvergne, they contained a simple bed and their walls were lined with blankets for warmth.

In the early part of the 18th century in Europe, the look of furniture went from heavy and masculine to feminine and light. In France, Baroque went out, a style called Regence made a peep, and in rolled the look called Rococo. In England, Queen Anne made a brief appearance, and then the lighter furniture became purely Georgian.

Rococo was playful and full of fancy; woodwork was ornamented

Opposite: *An 18th-century illustration of an 18th-century French* lit à l'Italienne, *assembled (Fig. 11) and disassembled to show its various parts.*

with seashells, flowers, rippling ribbons, dripping icicles, and similar frivolous touches. Bed frames were made mostly with mahogany, a wood that could accommodate the intricate carving called for by the new style.

English furniture makers—Chippendale, Hepplewhite, the brothers Adam, and Sheraton—began to be known by name. Chippendale, perhaps known best of all, made many interesting beds. Some looked like Gothic cathedrals; others brought Chinese pagodas to mind. Sheraton designed what he called a summer bed: two narrow beds lined up with space to walk between and covered by a single large tester.

And new types of beds appeared in France during the 17th and 18th centuries. The *lit d'ange*, or angel bed, had half a tester and no posts at its foot. The *duchesse* bed was similar, but its tester reached from the foot to the head. The *lit à la polonaise* had a headboard and a footboard of equal height. One contemporary source described over ninety variations. And the French started sticking their beds in alcoves that ranged in size from modest niches the size of the bed to great holes in the sides of rooms.

The second half of the 18th century saw furniture change once more. The new period was called Neoclassical; it lasted until Louis XVI lost his head (1793) and laid the foundation for the next great styles. The new look was influenced by the great European interest in some startling archaeological finds; one was the unashing of Pompeii.

During the 18th century, a number of things were happening to American beds. Those belonging to the affluent were reflecting the styles favored back in the Old World, especially England, each new look taking a few years to cross the ocean and take hold. The average colonial slept in a simpler bed, usually a four-poster that was decidedly New World in feeling. And while the well-to-do were sleeping on the Queen Annes and Chippendales, and others between their four posts, more adventurous types were chopping away at the frontier, building log cabins and beds to go inside them out of what they chopped away. A typical type was the jack bed: a single post set up on the ground about six feet from one cabin wall and about four feet from another; poles going from the post to the walls; slats placed across the poles to make a springy surface; a straw-filled sack placed on top.

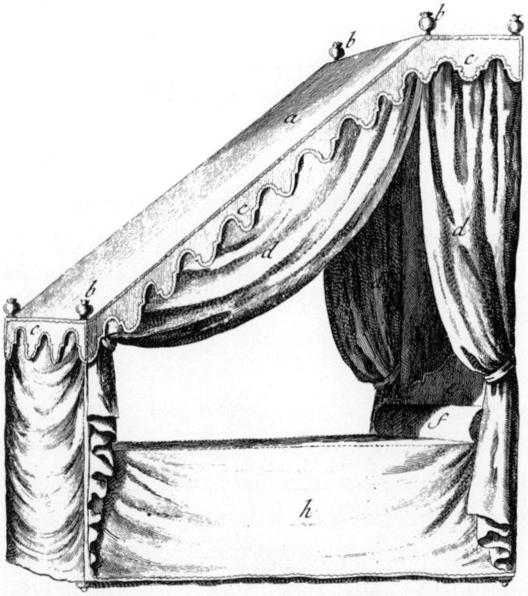

An 18th-century French dictionary illustration of a lit en tombeau, *a bed type common to most homes of the day. Its sloping canopy allowed for its space-saving placement against a stairway.*

The Shakers, the religious sect that first settled in New York State in

Beds in late-19th-century New York City were both humble and grand. Above: *The "beds" Jacob Riis captured with his camera in Happy Jack's 7 Cent Lodging House, an establishment on Pell Street similar to many on the Lower East Side that catered to indigent immigrants and others lacking the funds for better, were nothing more than narrow canvas strips affixed to endless beams.* Below: *Herter Brothers, a decorating firm with a list of clients that included the J. P. Morgans and the Vanderbilts, produced this impressive ebonized cherry wood "art furniture" bed with intricate marquetry decorations around 1880.*

1776, produced very beautiful, simple, and functional furniture, which they made for themselves and to sell. The Shaker bed was a simple frame with either no posts or very low posts, a rope foundation, and wheels that made it very easy to move the bed away from the wall to clean the floor.

Meanwhile, 18th-century mattresses improved dramatically. The shapeless sack of straw or cotton or wool that hadn't changed significantly for hundreds of years was gradually replaced by a more compact, hair-filled mattress with a shape similar to that of mattresses today.

Napoleon Bonaparte changed the map of the Continent and then the appearance of European furniture. The result was the French Empire, a furniture style of the same name, and beds that were grandiose, angular renditions of the couch-beds of the ancients, with the emphasis on the Egyptians. Golden palms, golden sphinxes, and crossed swords were typical adornments applied to the most exotic of woods. Curtains were frequently draped over crossed lances, giving quite permanent beds the appearance of being part of some great ancient general's open-air battlefield bedroom. The symmetrical quality of the Empire style created some other interesting beds. The *lit en bateau* looked like a boat; the *lit en corbeille*, a basket.

The English, who were also Nilophiles of some note, picked up on the style. In Germany and Austria, a heavier but less grand version of Empire was called Biedermeier. And in America, Empire-inspired sleigh beds appeared.

By 1830, Napoleon had been dead for nine years, the Empire style was out, Victoria was getting ready to come in for a long stay in Britain, and furniture makers everywhere were dredging the past for ideas. Rococo once again fluttered onto the furniture scene, followed by Gothic and Elizabethan revivals. In England, beds with great bulbous melon shapes carved into their posts became popular. Queen Anne and even the Greeks reappeared briefly.

Around 1880, a sensuous new style seemingly grew out of the mad mishmash of periods from the past. It was called Art Nouveau, and its beds were wrapped in a lush undergrowth of curvilinear plant life. It was a dreamlike fairy tale in which Mother Nature went erotically berserk, and it lasted into the 20th century, when the drought that was the First World War caused it to shrivel up and expire.

Right: *As depicted in a mid-19th-century periodical, the daily routine inside a French iron bed* (lits de fer) *factory.*

Below: *A "now-you-see-it-now-you-don't" bed, the Ta-Bed, was advertised in a 1923 women's magazine.*

Table by day—Bed by night
The patented Ta-Bed is both a superb mahogany or walnut finished Library Table and a full length luxurious bed combined—a wonderful saver of space and money. Saves rent of one room. Absolutely guaranteed. On easy terms from our dealers. Write for special offer.
TA-BED CORP., 310 Amer. Furn. Mart, Chicago, Ill.

A great boom in building beds out of metal was another feature of the 1800s. Factories on both sides of the Atlantic replaced cabinetmakers left and right, producing cast-iron and tubular brass beds by the thousands; the healthfulness of sleeping on metal was enthusiastically endorsed by a newly germ-conscious populace.

Between the middle of the 19th century and its end, European and American patent protections were granted for beds that turned into pianos, bathtubs, tables, vehicles, fireplaces, bookcases, fire escapes, and a bewildering assortment of equally unlikely objects. Devices for attaching cribs to beds, killing bedbugs, securing sheets and blankets, protecting the sleeper from mosquitoes, and preventing bed-wetting were developed. Hundreds of demented contraptions for waking up or warning heavy sleepers were dreamed up; most of these bed-related brainchildren stayed safely tucked away in the files of the Patent Office.

But all of the inventiveness and compulsion did lead to great advances with respect to that part of the bed which supports the mattress. Springy foundations of every description appeared—mesh screening resting on large supporting coils, thin chains crisscrossing, adjustable wires stretched on a metal frame, and hundreds of similar variations. The number of different coil designs alone is almost countless.

Perhaps the signal event in the world of the bed in the present century was the invention of the innerspring mattress, which took place in the 1920s. The boxspring, the seemingly inseparable companion of the innerspring mattress, wasn't a reality until shortly before World War II. The Harvard adjustable bed frame lifted both off the floor, and with the addition of a headboard to one end of this threesome, the Hollywood bed was born. The vast majority of Americans now sleep on just such a boxspring-innerspring mattress/metal frame/headboard combination. The development of the modern convertible sofa-bed, the invention of the electric blanket, and the reemergence of the 19th-century cowboy's bunkhouse bed as a juvenile bedroom furniture staple also took place in the 1920s.

Some interesting innovations of the past ten years have begun to have a considerable impact on Western sleeping habits. Water beds, for example, with their fluid-filled "puncture-proof" rubber mattresses, established a beachhead in the battle for bed buyers in the early '70s and have ridden a rising and falling tide of popularity ever since. Loft beds—platforms, usually carpenter-built or homemade and sometimes quite large, high enough off the floor to allow their space-starved urban owners

The idea of hiding a bed in another piece of furniture didn't originate in the 20th century, or even in the very inventive 19th. The mahogany, ash, birch, and white pine "deception bed" shown here (being both deceptive and honestly open) was made in Massachusetts between 1780 and 1790.

to walk under them when they aren't sleeping in them—are another fairly recent phenomenon. Platform beds—simple shallow boxes situated on slightly smaller supporting pedestals—are still another. The growing popularity of the latter two, since they do not take a boxspring, has prompted enterprising bedding manufacturers to develop specially designed foam mattresses and mattresses with innersprings encased in foam shells.

The great designers of the earlier part of this century—Mies van der Rohe, Le Corbusier, Charles Eames, and others—designed some really wonderful chairs, but they virtually ignored the bed. In the past decade or so, however, the bed has received much attention, and a whole new generation of inspired designers (especially European ones, with Italians leading the way) are again influencing what we sleep on.

What about beds in the years ahead? What's going to happen to them ten or twenty or two hundred and twenty years from now? Perhaps someone will come along and discover that we should have been sleeping on the ground all along. Maybe by the 22nd century we'll all be levitating, and taking our children to see all the odd artifacts—boxsprings and pillows and headboards and testers and mattresses and more—that used to fill up the ancient sleeping spaces of prelevitating *Homo sapiens*. Who's to say it won't happen? But if it does, chances are we'll still levitate in the same place every night, and whatever is levitating us will occupy some kind of container. It will surely have to have a name. Why not call it a bed?

BED OPTIONS

It may be observed, regrettably to be sure, that most of the earth's humans lead fairly optionless lives. The food on dinner tables, for example, in culture after culture varies very little from one day to the next. In the United States, on the other hand, the gastronomical options are astronomical. And the same can be said for choices in American beds.

But most Americans limit themselves to an uninteresting variety. Walk into any dwelling in any part of the nation—a house on a tree-lined Sun Belt street, a high-rise apartment in Seattle, a brownstone walk-up off Manhattan's Central Park, a condominium on Florida's Gulf Coast, a farmhouse in Nebraska—and the odds against your finding an unusual bed inside are high. What you will encounter instead in all likelihood is Hollywood bed (headboard/metal frame/mattress and boxspring) after Hollywood bed (headboard/metal frame/mattress and boxspring) after Hollywood bed (headboard/metal frame/mattress and boxspring), and so on.

The reason? Simple. Most people in need of a bed head straight for the nearest bed store, usually an establishment that sells one predictable thing only: Hollywood beds—with their (yawn) headboards, metal frames (yawn), mattresses, and (double yawn) boxsprings. An exciting change of pace might call for the daring addition of some sort of nondescript footboard to the end of the ubiquitous metal frame.

Fortunately, enough adventurous souls seek out interesting beds to keep the makers of interesting beds busy making interesting beds and the sellers of interesting beds, both old and new, selling them. Beds that disappear behind doors, bookcases, and walls; brass beds, antique ones and brand-new ones; beds that descend from the ceiling; beds that zip together with zippers; bunk beds of wood, aluminum, or steel; trundle, truckle, and hi-riser beds; all kinds of beds to make from kits; beds that turn into couches and chairs; antique beds from days gone by; antique reproductions that look just like originals; platform beds with drawers for

> The Haida Indians of the Queen Charlotte Islands (off the British Columbian coast) used to go to war quite often. Whenever the men paddled off in their canoes to do battle, the women would sleep for the first ten nights with their heads pointing in the bellicose paddlers' direction. But from the eleventh night on, they switched 180 degrees around, believing that doing so hastened the warriors' return.

storage; beds with four posts, two posts, high posts, low posts, and no posts; Shaker beds with wheels; contemporary beds that look like sculptures; rustic beds that look as if they grew out of the ground; beds that inflate and deflate; one-of-a-kind beds from fine woodworkers' shops; beds that slide out from under split-level platforms; water beds and beds filled with gel; beds that screw together from modular parts; beds made from cardboard; loft beds you crawl up and into; beds that vibrate; beds that elevate; beds that rotate; and even beds you roll up and put away in the morning—just some of the options open to the bed buyer who's brave.

All exercise requires time and some measure of effort. Exercising options is no exception. But exercise of any kind has its rewards, and the effort and time spent looking for a bed that's more than just another boring bed will be rewarded over and over again, night after unboring night.

Antique Beds

Every age leaves its own distinctive bed types behind, and although museums have most of the really old and most splendid ones, a considerable number of fine examples from a range of periods are still available to the contemporary buyer, sometimes at surprisingly affordable prices.

Unlike most other antique furniture types, an antique bed is seldom if ever bought simply to be placed in some spot in a room where it can be casually admired. A collector may acquire a collection of chairs, but few people build collections of beds. Beds demand to be used. They also take up considerable space. And then there is the problem of relative sizes; the dimensions of most antique bed frames bear little similarity to today's standard mattress, boxspring, and fitted sheet sizes. Consequently, beds are relative white elephants in the world of antiques, and bargains are to be found there by the individual with his or her heart set on a good old bed.

Two distinct advantages come with every antique bed. First, there's the considerable satisfaction of owning a piece of the past, a small part of a world different in so many ways from today's. And, on the more practi-

Tibetans sleep on beds that are very low to what to the rest of the world is the very high ground. House-dwellers on the 16,000-foot-high Tibetan Plateau sleep on small mattresses called *bōl-den*; they serve as seats during the day and, pushed together, as beds at night. Nomadic Tibetans sleep on the floors of their tents, on the skins of musk deer, sheep, stag, or chamois.

cal side, there's the knowledge that the value of one's bed is more likely to go up than down.

Antique dealers deal in antique beds and auction houses auction them off to the highest bidder. Once you've decided what kind of antique bed you want, it is a good idea to try both sources.

Some antique dealers, because of the problems previously mentioned, steer away from handling antique beds. Others simply lack the space to show them. But there are dealers who specialize in antique beds, or buy them to sell whenever they can. Ask antique dealers you meet if they know a fellow dealer who has antique beds. Look in the Yellow Pages. Check the classified ads and space ads in your local newspaper and in antique magazines. Or take a walk through a neighborhood where there are lots of shops. Many antique dealers keep "want lists," with the names of customers and their special desires. Get your want on a list.

Auction houses usually advertise approaching auction dates in local newspapers, and their display ads often contain fairly comprehensive lists of what will be offered. A day or two before the auction is held, potential bidders (which means anyone) are usually allowed to examine the items going up for auction. These exhibition days can be both fascinating and educational, and might even yield a bed to bid on.

A little caution should be exercised by anyone who has not participated in an auction before. Attending one or two auctions before actually jumping in to start bidding at one is a very good idea. When you feel you have the hang of it, decide what you want to spend on the bed you wish to bid on; then do your best to bring it in at that price, very close to it, or, if at all possible, for less. People have been known to sneak away quietly from an auction with merchandise they guiltily feel they've virtually stolen.

What can you do about fitting out an odd-sized antique bed with modern-day bedding? There are two possible choices. One, you can have custom bedding (mattress, boxspring, and fitted sheets) made to fit the bed. Weigh the cost of pursuing that course of action against the cost of the second: having the bed made physically larger or smaller, which usually requires the services of a carpenter or, better still, a person who specializes in this kind of alteration. Save the old parts and add the cost to the value of the bed.

The reindeer-herding mountain Lapps of Scandinavia's northernmost reaches have ideas about shoes. It is considered a disgrace, for example, to be seen with one's shoes untied. But that's not the half of it. If one eats with loose shoelaces, his father will die. If he eats while wearing only one shoe, the deceased will be his mother. When one Lapp sees another Lapp walking around without shoes, the first Lapp says, "You look like a dead person, with no shoes on." A part of the floor in a Lapp house is reserved for sleeping; it is covered with leafy branches in summer and twigs in winter. When the Lapps go to bed there, they leave their shoes on, so the evil creature known as the *Stollo* cannot pull the veins from their feet, which seems to be a pretty good reason.

There are sound sleepers and then there are sound sleepers. The Trukese of Truk Island in the South Pacific are sounder sleepers than most, and Trukese women (if what some people say is true) may be the soundest sleepers in the world. What's said is that if a Trukese male has designs of a sexual nature on a Trukese female who isn't likely to reciprocate, he may succeed all the same, simply by sneaking into her hut at night and taking his pleasure while she remains unaware in the depths of what may be the world's deepest sleep.

Antique Reproduction Beds

You can't find the antique bed you want in any antique shop. What you're looking for isn't likely to come up on your local auction block in the foreseeable future. Or the one you've found is perfect but priced for the Metropolitan Museum of Art, not you. What do you do? You might consider an old bed that's brand-new: a reproduction.

A reproduction—a good one, that is—follows the original historical piece from which it is copied in all matters of material, technique, and detail; in other words, it should be made today the way the original was made originally. Most of the reproduction beds being made today are copies of 18th-century American designs. A good Louis XIV *lit de parade* reproduction is as hard to find as an original Louis XIV *lit de parade*.

One of the great practical advantages reproduction beds offer is their availability in a range of contemporary bedding sizes. And, treated with the respect and care it deserves, a well-built 18th-century bed manufactured in the 20th century should be in pretty good shape (and quite valuable) well into the 22nd.

Cabinetmakers' and Fine Woodworkers' Beds

These often interchangeably used titles—cabinetmaker and woodworker—can be more than a little confusing. A cabinetmaker is invariably a woodworker, but a woodworker, fine or otherwise, is not necessarily a cabinetmaker. But if you let your fingers do the walking through any good-sized Yellow Pages and have them stop at either "Cabinet Makers" or "Woodworkers," you are likely to discover—among the cabinetmakers that make kitchen cabinets and nothing more, and the woodworkers that make the same—the names, addresses, and telephone numbers of individuals who, calling themselves either woodworkers or cabinetmakers, make very fine furniture. Perhaps even a bed or two that's very close to the sort of thing you've been looking for.

The number of fine woodworkers and cabinetmakers engaged in

creating new and original designs in furniture, and producing them in limited quantities, has grown dramatically over the past few years. Acquiring a bed made by such a craftsperson brings with it the gratifying knowledge that your patronage is helping to support and save an endangered species—the creative worker in wood.

Some woodworker/cabinetmakers make one-of-a-kind pieces, producing a unique design each time. Others may have just one bed that he or she makes in a variety of sizes on order. And then, of course, there's the exciting possibility of finding a woodworker who'll let you help him with the designing of a bed that's for nobody else but you.

The Kols of the western Indian state of Kolaba believe that iron has considerable protective powers. Kol women, for example, wear iron bracelets and rings of iron about their necks to ward away evil, while the sick keep iron close at hand to keep from getting any sicker. But even healthy Kols sometimes sleep with a piece of iron under their heads, and iron nails are often driven into all four corners of the simple wooden cots the Kols sleep on.

Concealed Beds

Convertible Sofas (and Chairs), Trundle Beds and Hi-risers, and Other Space-Saving Beds That Look Like Something Else or Completely Disappear When They're Not Being Beds

During the opening decades of the 19th century, inventors began improving on the hollow-bench beds of their ancestors by developing and patenting couches that concealed folding bed frames inside. These were the forerunners of today's familiar convertible sofas.

The medieval trundle bed (see "A Quick History of the Bed") is still with us. The term, applied in days of old to a bed separate from and unattached to its covering "mother" bed, is now generally used to refer to any couch (or bed) with a mattress-filled drawer that rolls out from beneath the sitting or primary sleeping level. A variation, the hi-riser, is a twin bed (or a couch) with a mattress-bearing drawer that rolls out, rises to the height of the top mattress (or couch cushion), and locks in place.

William Lawrence Murphy forever did away with the term used to describe a bed that lifts up and into an upright box. A counterbalancing spring system developed by Mr. Murphy just before the turn of the century, along with an upward-tilting bed frame that was bolted to the floor, turned the centuries-old press bed into the famous Murphy In-A-Dor Bed. New generations of Murphys are still making beds that gently

One name above all others—Murphy—almost instantly brings to mind beds that disappear. In these photographs a door conceals, reveals, and then disgorges a 1927 version of William Murphy's patented "In-A-Dor Bed."

descend from all sorts of boxes, and new generations of designers are continuing to find new places and ways to hide beds.

As primary sleeping options, convertible sofas, trundle beds, and hi-risers are generally poor choices, mostly because their mattresses and mattress-supporting frames seldom provide the comfort and body support of full-time beds. As occasional beds, though, to be pressed into service when an extra sleeping place is needed, they can be excellent—just how excellent depends, of course, on how excellently they are constructed. Unfortunately, most convertible sofas, trundle beds, and hi-risers are hardly attractive. There are, however and fortunately, some very noteworthy exceptions.

Loft Beds

The bedrooms in many one-bedroom apartments are so tiny that there's room in them for one bed and very little more. While these room-for-one-bed-bedroom apartments, especially those in older buildings, are notoriously short on floor space, they often have plenty of room between floor and ceiling. To fill this fortunate void has come the loft bed, a sleeping platform built high enough to create useful space underneath and up to and into which the sleeper climbs by means of a ladder.

Loft beds are seldom bought in stores. Most are one-of-a-kinds built by carpenters or by their owners. One telephone directory's "Beds—Loft & Platform—Custom Built" heading refers the reader to "Carpenters" and "Furniture Designers & Custom Builders."

If you should build a loft bed all by yourself, it will cost you no more than the materials used in its construction. If a carpenter or custom builder builds one for you, the price will be a combination of the cost of materials and the builder's charge for his (or her) labor. Most loftmakers will be more than happy to give a free estimate of the cost of building a sleeping loft, along with some possibly helpful suggestions about what kind of loft bed might best suit your particular space and needs.

And there are lots of different possibilities. There are small lofts, just big enough for sleeping on. Larger lofts may provide space enough for a mattress (a conventional one *sans* boxspring or a simple layer of foam rubber) and other pieces of "bedroom" furniture. Some loft beds are nearly as big as the rooms they're built into.

Apartment dwellers with lofty ideas should find out what their building's regulations regarding structural improvements are before they begin building. Some landlords forbid sleeping lofts outright. Other building owners will let you build one as long as they approve of the plan and/or you agree to leave it up (or take it down and with you) when you decide to move out. A free-standing loft bed, one that requires no attachment to the apartment's walls, should meet with any landlord's approval.

There is one point about loft beds worth considering. Hot air rises, and loft beds, being up where the hot air rises to, can be uncomfortably warm places to sleep during warm times in warmer climes. The ventilation in the part of the room where the loft bed is to be situated should therefore be considered. Building the loft near a window into which a fan can be placed (or at a comfortable distance from an air conditioner) is a very good idea. In winter months, hot air rising is of course a blessing instead of a bane.

Aside from the interesting things you can do *in* a sleeping loft, there are many creative and clever things you can do with the space *under* one. Closets, an office, bookshelves, a swing, a couch and some chairs—these are all good ideas. A kitchen would be a bad idea.

Falling out of a loft bed? It's something that almost never ever happens. But, if you often fall out of a normal bed, you might want to consider something else.

Brass Beds

Bedmakers began making beds of brass for the masses in England around 1830. Because of the nonrotting, nonflammable, and unchop-upable nature of the material they were made of, a surprising number of 19th-century and early 20th-century brass beds (as well as beds of iron, iron and brass, and brass with some other companion material) have survived to this day. The fashion for brass beds all but disappeared around a half a century ago, but in the past few years they have become very popular once again; a typical bed sold by Sears, Roebuck at the turn of the century for four or five dollars and change would fetch hundreds today. Brass beds are definitely chic, and it seems they will remain so for some time to come. As a result of this new interest in brass, dozens of fabricators of new brass beds—copies of old beds and new styles for new tastes—have sprung up to meet the demand.

A number of these manufacturers work by a simple formula: (1) Take some thin, inexpensive brass tubing; (2) bend some of the tubes and leave some of them straight; (3) stick them together, using paper-thin couplings; (4) slap on some lightweight, dentable, decorative doo-dads here and there; (5) polish the whole thing up so it looks like a million dollars; and (6) sell it for as close to that as possible. Fortunately, these brassy bedmakers are avoidable.

There's a brass word to keep in mind when entering any brass-bed maker's emporium; it's *casting*. If you should hear either *stamping* or *spinning* used as a substitute for *casting*, take it as a sign to make a beeline for the nearest exit. A cast brass part is made by pouring molten

---

Modern Yakuts are fairly ordinary rural Russians; they stay at home, raise cattle, and do a little farming. But it wasn't always so. A couple of generations or so ago, they led a much more rugged nomadic herding life and were known far and wide as the "iron men of Siberia," an appellation better understood when one considers what the typical on-the-move-in-the-middle-of-winter Yakut had to do to turn in each night without freezing. First, he made a fire and spread a horse blanket very close to it. Next, using his fur jacket as a cover and his saddle for a pillow, he lay down and waited until the heat of the fire caused him to perspire. He then plugged up his nose and ears with wads of fur and covered his face, leaving only a tiny hole near his mouth to breathe through. And thus, night after night, the Yakuti "iron men" slept out under the stars.

metal into an appropriately shaped mold, letting it cool, removing the hardened casting, and then finishing it off by hand, using a series of lathes and buffers until it's shiny and heavy and virtually indestructible. A stamping or spinning, on the other hand, is made by forming a thin (sometimes very thin) sheet of brass around a form. Such brass parts are every bit as bright and shiny as their cast brass cousins, but they're also very fragile and highly dentable. When buying a brass bed—old or new—give all its parts a critical tap or two; you will be able to hear just how solid an investment your bed will be. The parts of the bed that should be cast are the knobs that decorate and cap off tube ends and the couplings that join sections of tubing together.

And don't be fooled by the term *solid brass*; it can be applied to any brass bed, even a paper-thin one, just as long as it's made of brass and not brass shaped around some other metal.

Avoid brass headboards and footboards that hook up feebly to a standard metal bed frame. Elements attached in this manner are often wobbly and detract from the solid feeling a good brass bed should impart. Better brass-bed makers have devised ingenious new systems for connecting the foot of the bed to the head, and each to the part that holds the bedding. Look for these important features.

If it's an antique brass bed you want, shop as carefully for it as you would for a new one; look for the same pros, the same cons. And watch out for wildly inflated prices.

"Can't I stay up just a little bit longer?" is one question a Tiv child is never heard asking his or her parents. The Tiv, a people living along the Benue River in northern Nigeria, have no fixed hours for sleeping: they go to bed whenever they feel like it, day or night. Tiv children are never encouraged to take naps or go to bed at any particular time, for a Tiv village is as active at 3 A.M. as it is at high noon.

The bed a Tiv sleeps on—when a Tiv gets around to going to sleep—is a simple yet impressive affair. Called a *kpande*, it's a wide plank supported on four short stubby legs, the whole being hewn from a single solid piece of wood.

Contemporary Beds

Every new bed is, speaking very strictly, a contemporary bed, even when it's a reproduction of a bed that's hundreds of years old. But some beds are decidedly more contemporary than others, and the term is generally applied to beds designed by professional designers along the lines of any of several prevailing contemporary styles. Beds currently being called contemporary are fabricated from stainless steel, leather, plastics, all kinds of woods, Formica, chrome, canvas, aluminum, and endless combinations of these and similar materials. Designs range from the stoically minimal to the enthusiastically overstuffed and upholstered, and devilishly clever modular systems abound. In short, there are plenty of interesting options for those who opt for a contemporary bed. But before exercising any particular option, some questions should be asked about it.

Who designed the bed? There is some good contemporary furniture design, and there is much bad. Innocuously bad contemporary furniture is often derisively labeled "modern"; the really hideous stuff is, with doubled derision, anagramatically dubbed "modren." While individual tastes and opinions do count for something, it is generally agreed that the vast majority of well-designed contemporary beds are designed by talented professionals who spend all, or most, of their time designing contemporary furniture. Most of today's best designers are Europeans working in Europe, with Italians definitely dominating. Fortunately, though, the ranks of talented American furniture designers are steadily swelling. Beware of no-name "designer" furniture. One furniture industry spokesman surprisingly admits that, by his estimation, only 30 percent of the furniture manufactured in the United States is designed by professionals. So, ask who designed the bed you desire. Find out something about him or her. If you ask who the designer of a "designer" bed is and the seller has no answer, it may be a sign that you have designs on the wrong bed.

How well is the bed made? Be especially wary of inexpensive contemporary beds that may, while looking like quality products of the very latest technology, actually be very primitive in their construction. A sparkling exterior layer of Formica, leather (or what looks like leather), or stainless steel can very successfully disguise an interior framework that might not be particularly sound. Superstreamlined futuristic beds, whatever their price, should be carefully examined, both inside and out, to make sure they are built solidly enough to have a reasonable chance of surviving until the time in which they look like they belong. Inspect, if you can, the bed's interior parts. If the frame is made of wood, does it look like worthy wood? If it's metal, is it more than just one of those inexpensive standard types hiding under a snazzy covering? How sophisticated is the joinery? Are screws or bolts used? Do they seem up to the job of holding the bed together? Does everything feel good and tight? When you apply reasonable force to various parts of the frame, is there any noticeable wobble? How well is any surface covering attached to the more solid parts of the bed? Look for tiny details that might reveal the bed's soundness, or lack of it.

Will you get tired of this bed? Is it a whim or an impulse, or will your love for it last a long, long time? It's a question that should be asked, and given more than just a little thought. It's a question, in fact, that should be asked about any bed, contemporary or not.

Platform Beds

The Jivaro Indians of Ecuador's rain forest are famous the world over for the shrinking of heads, but almost no one knows that they sleep on shrunken beds. The simple pole-elevated platforms Jivaros sleep on are only about four feet long and support no more than their trunks and heads. But their legs don't dangle; they're supported by a bar, placed on two forked sticks, on which the Jivaro places his heels. On the ground beneath the bar a fire is kept going, warming the sleeper's feet as its smoke keeps away the mosquitoes.

In its simplest form, a platform bed is nothing more than a shallow, mattress-sized box resting on a narrower and shorter foot-high-or-so pedestal. Fancier (and correspondingly costlier) variations have nightstands, bookcases, or entire wall systems built around their heads.

The first platform beds were made in Scandinavia during the 1930s. In the past few years they have become very popular here (especially on the East Coast), and a number of simple factors seem to account for all the interest. They are fairly inexpensive, especially when made from less expensive materials. They are simple in design, making them adaptable to a wide range of interiors. They are light and portable, which makes them ideal for an increasingly mobile population. They are very available; platform-bed makers are now plentiful.

Platform beds do not require boxsprings; that adds to their appeal. Most platform manufacturers also sell mattresses to fit. And perhaps the best evidence of the platform bed's success is the fact that almost every major bedding manufacturer has now developed special mattresses designed just for them.

Do-It-Yourself Beds

There once was a time (a long, long time ago) when every possession was made by its possessor. Not quite so long ago, people still made most of the things they had. But it eventually came to pass that almost everything we surrounded ourselves with was made for us by others, and it looked as if the time would come when we would produce nothing that we own on our own. But that never happened. Today, a growing number of crafty individuals are putting a lot of time and effort back into making all sorts of items for themselves, including some very interesting beds.

Why not build yourself a bed? A bed, after all, isn't all that complicated. Just think about all the things that are really beyond most of our individual do-it-yourself abilities—putting together an automobile or a food processor or a typewriter, for example. Compare making any one of them to building a simple platform for sleeping.

A bed can be built from scratch—designed, planned, and constructed by its creative maker. For the less adventurous there are detailed plans to follow. Kits requiring only simple tools and minimal skills provide a measure of do-it-yourself satisfaction.

If you possess no skills to speak of, perhaps you should consider acquiring some. There are schools of woodworking where the student usually works on a specific project of his or her choosing: make that project a bed. You could end up with two things: new skills and a new bed you made all by yourself.

Water Beds and Air Beds

> Some Iranians believe that if you place your clothes above your bed you will have a troubled sleep. On the other hand, if you put your pants under your head, any bad dreams you might have will not happen.

When the history of the bed is rewritten 200 or so years from now, the water bed may warrant a whole chapter, or only a footnote. Whether it continues to ride the crest of its present wave of popularity or whether interest ebbs away is something only the future can tell.

A water bed consists of a heavy-duty vinyl mattress-shaped bag containing a lot of water and enclosed in a strong frame, usually a fairly simple wooden one. Between the frame and the water mattress a safety liner guards against any possible outflow should a rare leak occur. Between the underside of the mattress and the retaining frame a heating unit serves to prevent condensation on the outside of the water bag, and also keeps the sleeper from freezing to death.

A few craftsmen started the water-bed business back around the turn of the '70s; now many major conventional mattress manufacturers are in the act. A large number of majors are now producing what they call "hybrids"—water-bed mattresses that consist of water bags in foam shells encased in vinyl. These are covered with conventional ticking so that they look just like conventional innerspring mattresses. Some manufacturers are even producing ersatz "boxspring" bases to go under their hybrids.

Many flotation enthusiasts insist that their back problems have been forever cured. Others tell of vastly improved sex lives, and still others say they just get seasick from the wave motion. (Some newer water beds feature internal chambers or baffles that reduce the lateral movement of water inside.) Perhaps the least appealing aspect of the water bed is the bed frame most water beds usually come in. The California-van-school-of-interior-design look is the major one; blowtorch-antiqued and meat-ax-distressed wood frames with genuine leather-look vinyl upholstery reminiscent of cheap rumpus room barrail cushions is a popular style. Velour side rails and fake fur spreads are also quite popular. Until well-designed water-bed frames become generally available, the real future of the water bed will be hard to assess.

The air mattress, a 19th-century novelty making a comeback on the West Coast, is the newest entry in the competition for the bed buyer's dollars. Most air mattresses intended for every-night use are little more than overblown versions of the familiar inflatable cushions used by campers and beachgoers. On the positive side, inflated air mattresses weigh only around twenty pounds; inflate quickly with a canister of compressed air, a bicycle pump, or conventional hair dryer; remain at room temperature; and require no special frame to contain them.

There's some strange bedtime palaver in the onetime land of the Pahlavis. To make sure they don't oversleep in the morning, some Iranians put their head on their pillow and then, addressing it, say, "May the miller, the customs officer, and the washer of the dead fall on you if you do not wake me early." It can be presumed that the miller, the customs officer, and the washer of the dead say something else to their alarm-clock-pillows.

Certain natives of Malaysia on the South China Sea also get double duty from their pillows. "Heigh! O Scribes of Solomon, I must sleep! Do you watch? If anyone, good or bad, comes here, do not hide or seek cover, but call me with all speed. There is but one God and Mohammed is the prophet," they say to them three times, then slap them three times, breathe over them three times, and go to sleep.

Unusual Beds

Some people have a superstrong streak of rugged individualism, a great sense of self-expression, a powerful need to be noticed, an insatiable appetite for the abnormal and outrageous, an overwhelming desire to be different, or a terrific sense of humor. For these diehard eccentrics and helpless nonconformists, only a unique bed will do.

Helpful suggestions to the buyer of a bizarre bed: (1) check to be doubly sure it's as sleepworthy as it is unusual, and (2) question your motives for buying such a bed and, considering the answer, try to assess how long it will be before the novelty fades away.

Mattresses and Mattress Foundations

Until recently, selecting a mattress (or a mattress/boxspring foundation combination, called "a full set of bedding" by the industry) was a fairly simple matter. But that's all changed in the past few years; it's not so easy anymore to decide on what kind of mattress or mattress/foundation combination to buy. A number of factors have contributed to the confusion: the advent of the low-profile bed look, of which the most dramatic example is the platform bed; the appearance of the water bed, which obviously doesn't require a traditional mattress; the controversy surrounding whether a soft mattress or a firm one is better for sleeping; and the question in some people's minds of whether a boxspring is a necessity or a waste of time. As a result, there is a myriad of different mattress types to choose from today.

The most popular mattress type is still the innerspring—a set of springs in any one of hundreds of configurations sandwiched between layers of cushioning and insulating material and enclosed in a fabric case. The layers of upholstery are kept from shifting by quilting them, or by joining them by means of regularly spaced buttons to the top covering layer, called the "ticking." The more coils a spring has, say manufacturers of mattresses with lots of coils, the better it is for sleeping on. Better still, say manufacturers of mattresses with lots of coils contained in individual fabric pockets, are mattresses with individually pocketed coils. A good mattress, say these manufacturers, should last between ten and fifteen years, depending on whether it's one of their less expensive models or one from the top of the line, and, any manufacturer worth his coils will invariably add before anyone has a chance to ask, provided the user uses it atop a life-extending boxspring foundation.

The Kurds, who live in a region called Kurdistan, which takes up parts of Turkey, Iraq, and Iran, rise above the summer heat by moving beds and bedding to their roofs. Branch fences built around the edge of the roof protect the women from the gaze of outsiders.

And in the Siwa Oasis, the Palm Springs of western Egypt near the Libyan frontier, the people sleep on top of their houses with their faces shielded from the moon, because they believe moonlight shining on sleeping faces causes madness.

The low-profile platform bed (which would look very strange and high-profile with a mattress plus boxspring on it) was the first major development in beds to call into question prevailing bedding wisdom. Soon after its introduction, bedding manufacturers deemed the platform bed a poor idea, stating that its hard mattress deck was torture to conventional innerspring mattresses. Platform bed enthusiasts paid no mind and employed conventional mattresses or thick layers of foam. Platform beds and other boxspringless low-profile beds became very popular, and manufacturers finally deemed it necessary for their own survival to create mattresses especially made for platform beds. Some of them developed mattresses with spring systems that were greatly reduced in size and encased in a thicker upholstery made mostly of foam. Others opted for 100 percent foam, using different types and numbers of layers. All-foam and innerspring/foam combination mattresses are therefore now among the options available to today's mattress buyer.

But there's more profit in boxsprings than in mattresses, which are much more labor-intensive and therefore more expensive to make, so manufacturers (and retailers, too) are loath to see them slip into bedding history. A number of casegoods makers (the bedding industry term for companies that make beds), sensing the need to satisfy mattress manufacturers, retailers, and consumers who don't want to see the boxspring die, have come out with low-profile "platform" beds, called "sandbox" beds, into which a boxspring slips unnoticed. The one possible flaw in this design is the assumption that people want their boxsprings hidden from view. Obviously disagreeing with that thinking, another casegoods firm unveiled an innovation that had even a lot of bedding industry people puzzled: an honest-to-goodness boxspringless platform bed with a base that sports false boxspring sides that make it look as if what your bedspread covers up is a genuine boxspring.

Some critics say that even if it does add a year or two to the life of a mattress, a boxspring isn't worth the added expense. Why spend money for a mattress and boxspring set that will last around twelve years, when you can spend approximately the same amount for two mattresses that will each last ten years for a total use time of twenty years? Doesn't that add up to eight years more than a mattress with boxspring can offer? Manufacturers counter with the need to turn a mattress more often if it

A bird with one terrible reputation is the olima, the name the agricultural Tarahumara Indians have given the great horned owl (*Bubo virginianus*), which flies around at night snatching small animals and even unwary cattle. In the winter, the Tarahumara retire to caves in the canyons that cut deeply through their high plateau in southern Chihuahua, in northern Mexico. There they sleep (on shelves called *kuhubela*, made by placing boards on crossed tree saplings) with their mouths tightly closed, because the olima also snatches the souls of the sleeping. Seeing a shooting star, a Tarahumara says, "There it goes, taking a soul," meaning that an olima has removed the soul from someone foolishly sleeping with his mouth open.

doesn't have the spring and cushion of a boxspring under it. That may or may not put the ball back in the critics' court.

The hardness of a mattress is another area of debate. Back doctors frequently prescribed very firm mattresses for their patients, and some went so far as to say that hard mattresses were better for everyone. The mattress industry responded with surprising speed. Undentable slabs in all the standard sizes with super-supporting springs and extra-hard upholstery were the result. It wasn't too long before cries of "Too hard!" were heard from a growing number of customers, so a new generation of "soft but firm" mattresses are with us now.

Aware of their proven track record for predicting future trends in the industry, the National Association of Bedding Manufacturers queried its manufacturer and retailer members for their views on what the future holds for mattresses and mattress foundations. Here are some of the responses as they were reported in *Bedding*, the organ of the NABM:

"I expect future bedding to contain less steel and more synthetic materials."

"It seems to me that new forms of inflatable mattresses will continue to appear and achieve some buying recognition. . . . Although the waterbed is probably not a final form, it represents an important breakthrough."

"I believe the foams will get stronger. People have been introduced to foam in hotels and campers and they like its practicality."

"Science will make available 'springless' mattresses and boxsprings; lack of weight psychologically adversely affected consumers' thinking in the case of polyurethane and rubber."

"The only type of technology that I could foresee changing the entire population's sleeping habits would be some type of supporting air jet streams that would suspend sleepers 6″ to 18″ off the floor through air pressure."

"The boxspring in its current form will be much less important. It will be replaced by other foundations—platform beds, foundations that are lower priced, that can become a greater part of the bed 'fashion.'"

"More and more casegoods manufacturers are showing and making low platform beds which obviate the use of boxsprings. . . . The lattice type of foundation popular in Europe could have appeal to our younger generation."

"For the long range, I see the possible demise of the boxspring as we know it today. This will be due to the fashion trend, and the need for a more multi-functional bedroom."

"The foundation . . . will change in two ways: into a better looking and probably upholstered platform bed, and probably a change in the spring construction of the foundation. That is to say, some sort of material that reacts like springs but isn't."

"The boxspring will likely evolve to a product only remotely similar to today's boxspring. Space is now so dear that the cubic area beneath the mattress will be exploited for other purposes besides sheer mattress support."

Mattresses are manufactured in fairly standard sizes, with one-inch discrepancies being the most frequently encountered. In the following chart, when two figures are given for one dimension, the one given first is the more standard:

Size Designation	*Dimensions (in inches)*
Cot	30 × 75
Divan	33 × 75
Twin	39 × 75 or 76
Twin, extra-long	39 × 80
Full (or Double)	54 × 75 or 76
Full, extra-long	54 × 80
Queen	60 × 80
King	76 or 78 × 80
California King	76 or 78 × 84

Prices

Price is sometimes no object, but every object has a price; more often than not, it's a price that's going up. Furniture prices, including those for beds, are no exception, and therefore the prices mentioned throughout this book should not be taken too literally.

UNITED STATES PATENT OFFICE.

RAY WERNER, OF SAN FRANCISCO, CALIFORNIA.

COMBINED PNEUMATIC MATTRESS AND GARMENT.

1,316,469. Specification of Letters Patent. Patented Sept. 16, 1919.

Fig. 1.

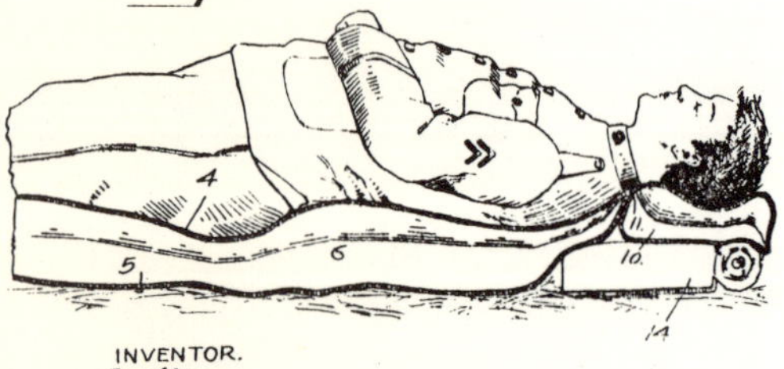

INVENTOR.

Ray Werner

By [illegible]

Atty.

Fig. 2.

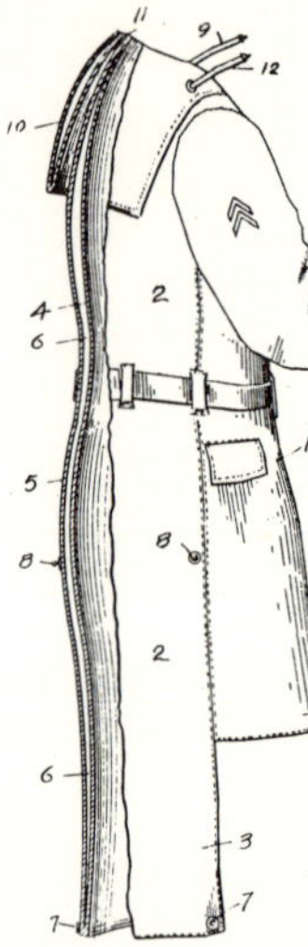

Fig. 3.

To all whom it may concern:

Be it known that I, Mrs. RAY WERNER, a citizen of the United States, residing in the city and county of San Francisco and State of California, have invented a certain new and useful Improvement in Combined Pneumatic Mattresses and Garments, of which the following is a specification.

My invention relates to improvements in garments wherein the back portion is formed with an air tight compartment and provided with an inflatable collar to be used as a pillow, said compartment and collar having separate inflating means whereby each may be inflated independently of the other.

The primary object of my invention is to provide a garment, the back of which may be inflated to provide a resilient support for the body of the wearer without removing the garment thus providing a greater comfort while reclining in a recumbent position.

A further object of the present invention is to provide a garment of the character described having an inflatable back portion provided with a folded train which may be unfolded and inflated with the remainder of said back portion to provide a resilient support of suitable length.

It is also an object of the invention to provide a separate inflatable compartment attached to the back of the garment which may be used as a pillow.

I accomplish these several features by means of the device disclosed in the drawings forming a part of the present specification wherein like characters of reference are used to designate similar parts throughout the said specification and drawings, and in which—

Figure 1 is a broken sectional view of my improved garment as applied to the person and in a recumbent position;

Fig. 2 is a broken perspective view of the garment when worn in an inoperative position; and

Fig. 3 is a broken side elevation of a garment partly in section disclosing the train unfolded and ready for inflation.

Referring to the drawings the numeral 1 is used to designate in general a garment, which, in the present instance, is depicted in the form of a military overcoat, but it should be understood that the present invention may be applied to any form of outer garment generally used for protection from the elements.

124 BEDS

A 19th-Century *Lit à la Polonaise*

This extremely unusual and rare bed, a Dutch marquetry *lit à la polonaise* from the first quarter of the 19th century, could have been yours if you had attended the January 31, 1975, auction at the New York auction house of Sotheby Parke Bernet (980 Madison Avenue, New York, N.Y. 10021), where it was sold. The pre-auction estimate of what one might expect to have to bid for it was between $2,000 and $3,000. A lucky bidder snapped it up for $1,800.

Two Senufo Beds

The Senufo, a major tribal people of the Ivory Coast in West Africa, carve their four-legged wooden beds from solid pieces of native hardwood. More interesting even than that is the fact that anyone looking for something truly different in a bed can actually buy one—without having to make the trip to the Dark Continent. Craft Caravan, an importer of all kinds of unusual African artifacts, located at 127 Spring Street, New York, N.Y. 10012, will be happy to sell one to you.

The two beds shown here are both adult size, the larger of the two being for an adult somewhat higher up on the Senufo social ladder. It's 25 inches wide, 16 inches high, and 91 inches long, with the "pillow" adding another 7 inches to the height. The smaller bed is 13 inches wide, 6 inches high, and 70 inches long; the pillow is 4 inches high. The larger bed's price is $1,800. The smaller one is $400. If you want to add a mattress, it will have to be a custom-made one.

The Anfibio sofa-bed looks like a perfectly normal well-stuffed sofa when its arm-backrest section is properly strapped into place. But the aptness of its name becomes much more apparent when Anfibio's straps are undone and the sofa is allowed to turn into something that looks like an inflatable craft abandoned on a beach by frogmen. Closed, it measures 94½ inches wide by 38½ inches deep by 25½ inches high. Opened up and ready to drift you off into a sea of dreams, it measures 94½ inches long by 78 inches wide by 13 inches high. The sleeping area is 58 inches by 74 inches. In 100 percent linen (white, natural, black, or brown) Anfibio sells for $2,286; in leather (black, dark brown, or terra cotta) it sells for $3,472. Anfibio's designer is Alessandro Becchi. International Contract Furnishings Inc., 145 East 57th Street, New York, N.Y. 10022, sells the Anfibio sofa-bed, through interior designers, decorators, and architects only.

The Anfibio Sofa-bed

Above: *Italian designer Alessandro Becchi's Anfibio sofa-bed, as a sofa.*

Right: *The Anfibio sofa-bed, opened up and ready for casting off.*

Nathan Young has adopted the pattern of a sunburst as his personal design signature. This bed, made of laminations of red oak, is an example of the actor-turned-cabinetmaker's use of the motif. The queen-size bed shown sells for $650. Other sizes (at other prices) are available, as are matching pieces you can fill up a bedroom with until it's sunbursting at the seams.

Nathan Young's designs can be seen in his showroom at 58 Carmine Street, New York, N.Y. 10014.

Nathan Young's "Sunburst" Bed

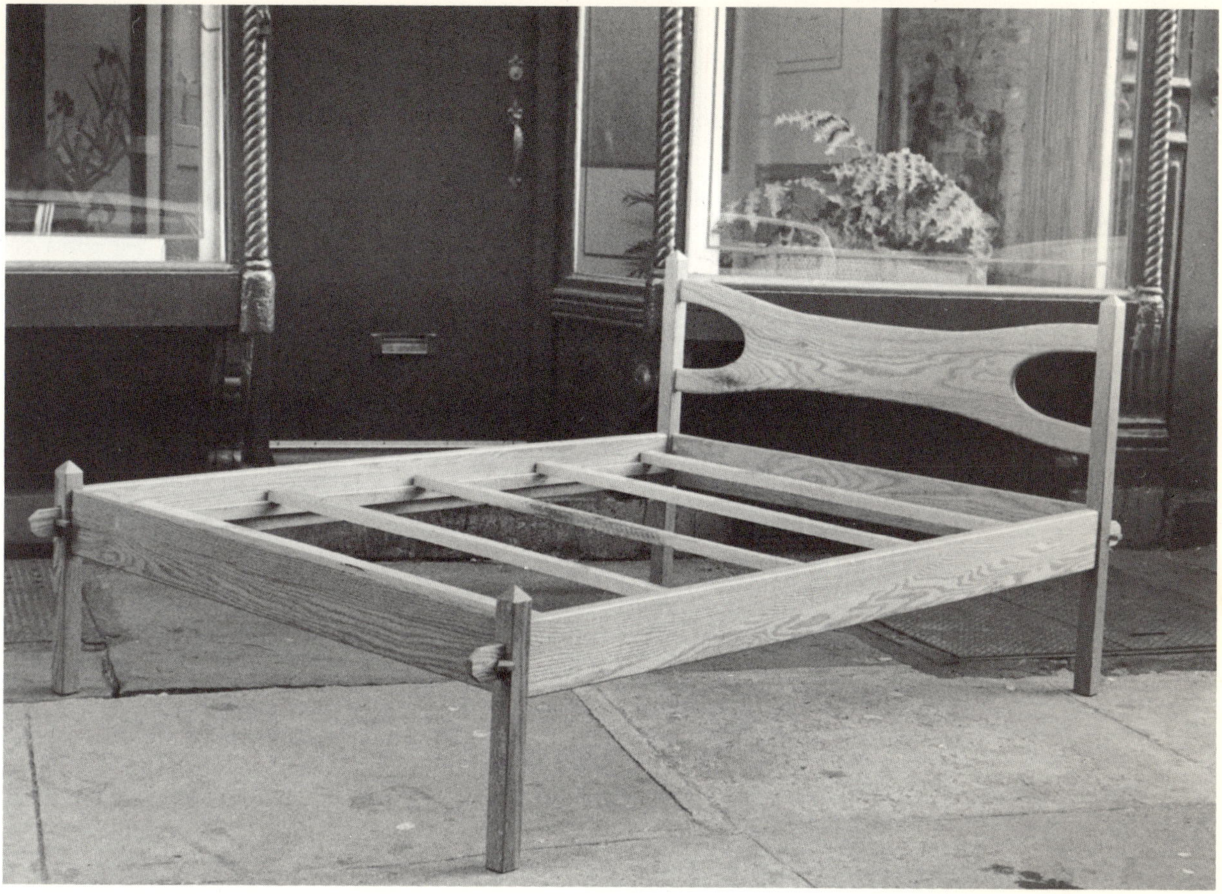

Detail showing the wedged through-tenon joinery that permits disassembling for storage or transporting.

A Red Oak Bed by Cabinetmaker Peter Korn

This red oak double bed with wedged through-tenon joints was handcrafted by cabinetmaker Peter Korn. Korn is best known for an award-winning and patented collapsible music stand design, but his beds are well worth what he asks for them. This one is $500. In cherry it's $550. For storing or shipping, it breaks down into four main pieces. The time between ordering a Peter Korn bed and getting it, depending on how busy he is, is between two and six months. Custom bed orders are also welcomed by the Philadelphia-born woodworker, whose gallery and workshop are located at 236 Elizabeth Street, New York, N.Y. 10012.

Two Jacobean Tester Bed Reproductions

Trouvailles, Inc. (305 East 63rd Street, New York, N.Y. 10021), will "reproduce these two authentic 17th-century antique beds exactly in detail, in any dimensions required to custom order." The Wrentham Four Poster Bed (left) is 40 inches (102 cm) wide by 75 inches (190 cm) long by 72 inches (183 cm) high. The Worcester "B" Four Poster Bed (right) is 54 inches (137 cm) wide by 81 inches (206 cm) long by 78 inches (198 cm) high. Both are acid oak. Prices are available on request.

A 19th-Century Mahogany Daybed

It was estimated that on April 27, 1977, Lot 919, a "classical brass-mounted mahogany daybed, New York, c. 1815," would fetch from $1,000 to $1,500 for the person who consigned it to be auctioned at Sotheby Parke Bernet, the New York auction house. "Each upright with a gilt-metal mount in the form of stylized leafage and *rinceaux* above a conformingly inlaid skirt; on rectangular legs ending in molded feet. Feet repaired. Length 6 feet 10 inches (2.08 m)," read the auction catalog description. The buyer must have been as delighted as the seller was not, because the top and winning bid was only $600.

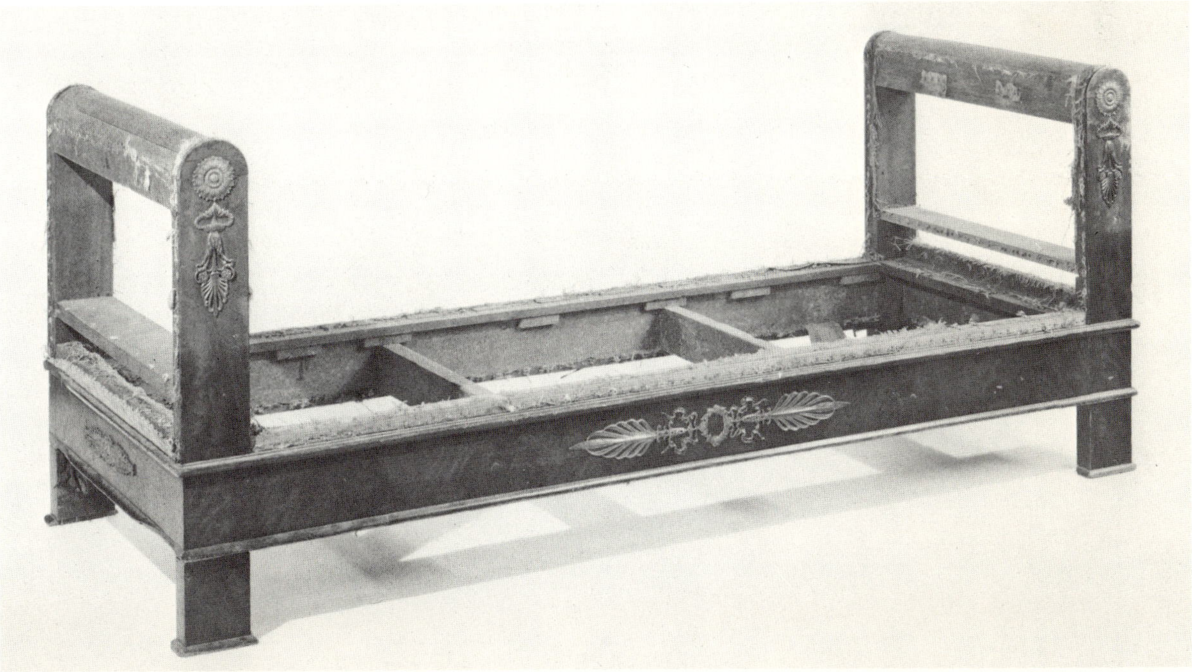

Bunk Bed Plans to Send For

You can make this pair of bunk beds from full-sized furniture plans from Furniture Designs, 1425 Sherman Avenue, Evanston, Ill. 60201. Here's how the Furniture Designs catalog of plans describes these beds: "Here is a plan that is in great demand. It is a fine wood turning project in sturdy Early American styling designed to withstand hard usage. Can be reassembled as a pair of twin beds by using an end of the lower bunk and an end of the upper bunk. The plan shows the easy-to-make moveable ladder and guard rail. Any standard twin-size mattresses can be used with these beds. Size assembled as Bunk Beds: 42½ inches × 83 inches × 63¼ inches high."

This is Furniture Designs plan 171, and it's $7. For more information about Furniture Designs furniture plans, see page 108. See also page 71.

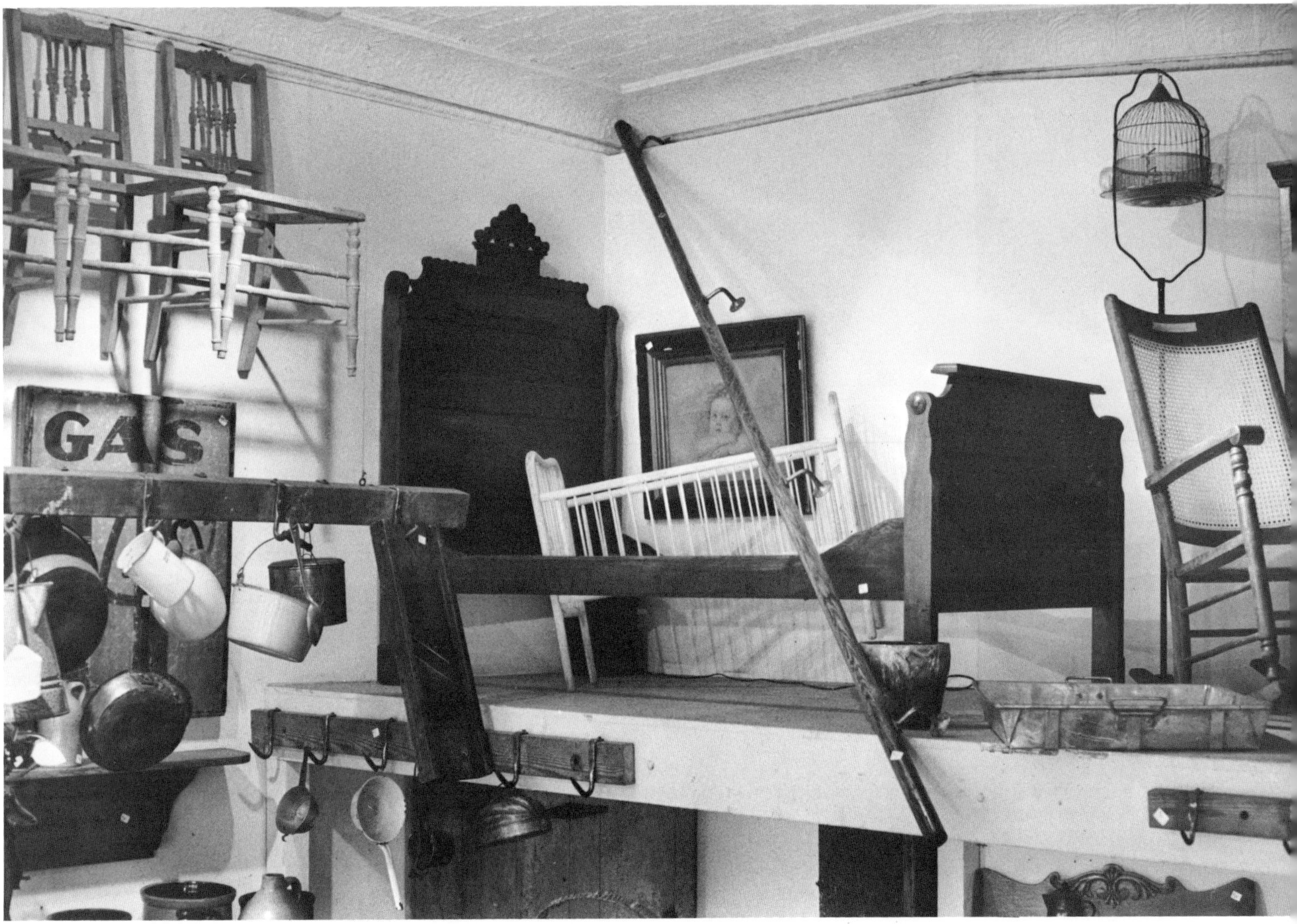

An Antique Victorian Walnut Bed

Nestling snugly in a corner of a loft at Coccabahli Antiques, 292 Columbus Avenue, New York, N.Y. 10023, is an American Victorian walnut bed. This last-half-of-the-last-century single bed was selling for $450.

A Japanese Futon Bed

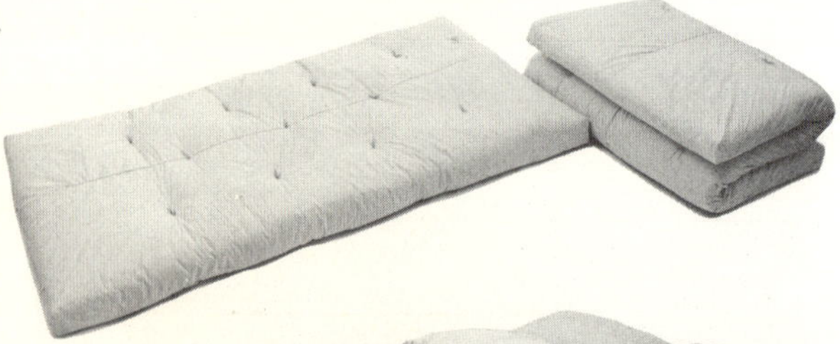

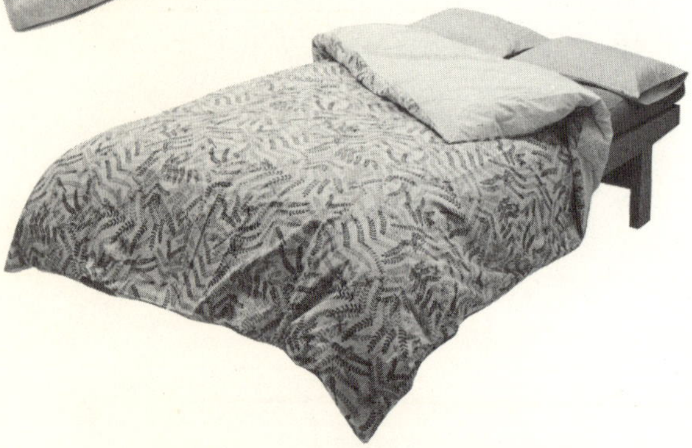

Top: *The bed is constructed with dovetail joints and can be easily disassembled without the use of tools; no hardware is used in its construction.*

Center: *The Japanese futon mattress, opened flat and closed for storing.*

Bottom: *Shinera's bed frame with futon mattress, buckwheat-hull-stuffed pillows, and colorful comforter on top.*

The maple bed frame with poplar slats is something Shinera has just started making, but they've been making "futon" mattresses for quite some time. For those who aren't familiar with this oriental bed form, Shinera explains:

"For centuries in the Orient, beds and pillows have been made using simple design principles to provide healthful sleep. 'Futon' mattresses were thin mats, filled with cotton batting and encased in colored cotton fabrics. During the day futons were folded and stored; at night they were rolled out on 'Tatami' (rice straw) mats for sleeping. The natural materials provided maximum comfort and the unique construction gave excellent support to the back and spine. . . .

"Eight layers of cotton batting are used [in the futons Shinera makes] so that the futons are comfortably thick (about six inches). Each futon has evenly spaced tufts, done with rug yarn, pulled through the mattresses and tied like a quilt. The tufting secures the batting, top and bottom, to the muslin case. . . .

"Futons are extremely comfortable and give excellent back support because they never sag. They can be used directly on the floor and can be rolled up or folded during the day to provide more usable floor space. They can also be placed on a platform. . . . Sizes for all futons are the same as standard mattresses and are compatible with standard bed frames and fitted bed linens."

Special sizes can be made on order for children's futons, baby's cribs, vans and campers, floor couches, and as exercise mats.

Shinera sells futons and maple bed frames with poplar slats by mail. Futon prices, which do not include shipping, are: $53 for a twin or single (39 by 75 inches); $58 for a three-quarter (48 by 75 inches); $68 for a double (54 by 75 inches); and $80 for a queen (60 by 80 inches). The bed frames that fit under the four sizes of futons are $225, $235, $245, and $255, respectively.

Shinera also sells two different kinds of covers for their futon mattresses and explains why they are a good idea: "Removable, colored covers provide protection for your futon and create an attractive floor couch. The cover [100 percent cotton] is designed to pull over the futon and close with fabric ties on one end. . . . Muslin covers for the futons pull on like a pillowcase and tie at one end. Since the futon, like a regular

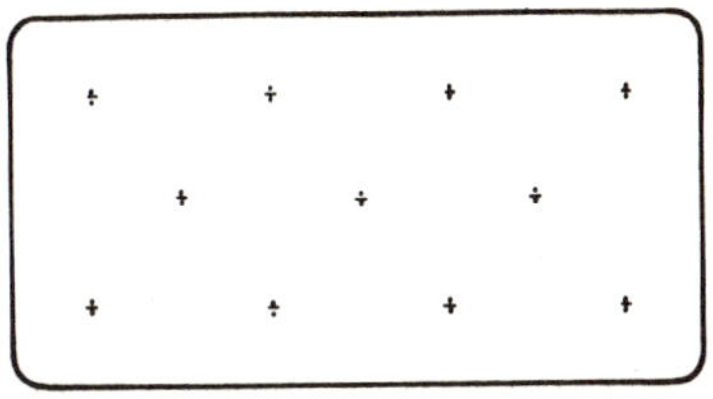

Single futon (39 by 75 inches).

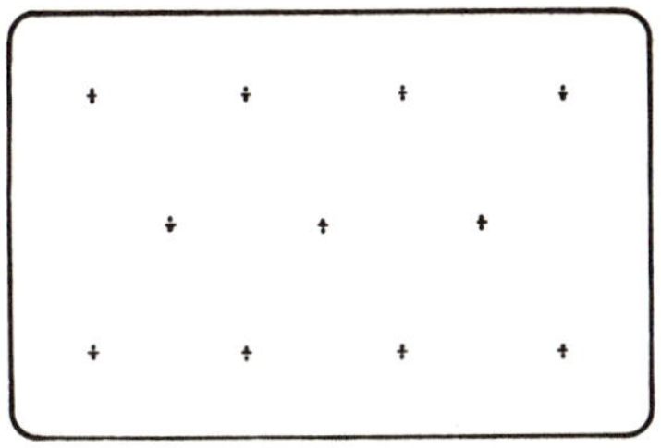

Three-quarter futon (48 by 75 inches).

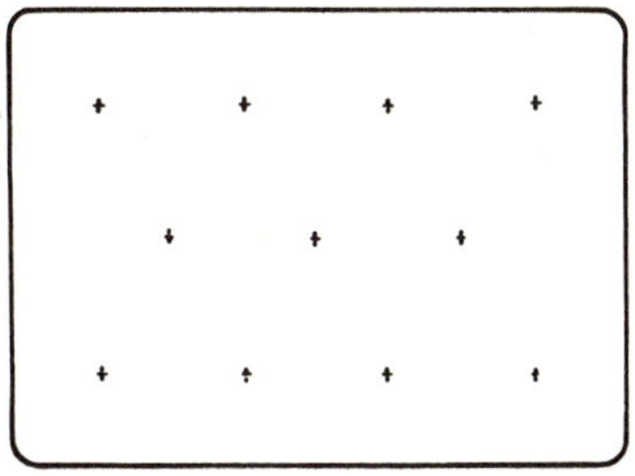

Double futon (54 by 75 inches).

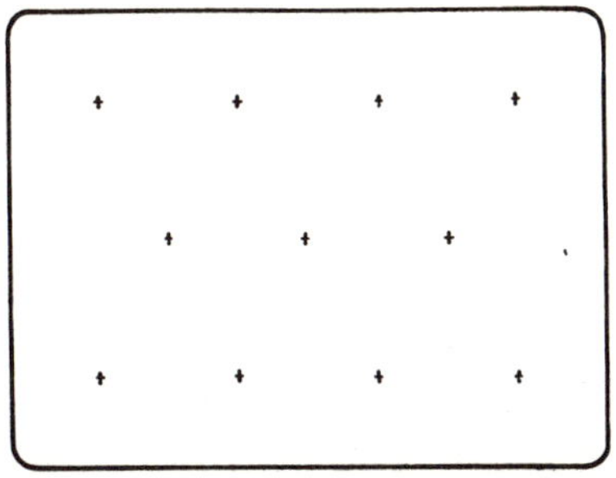

Queen-size futon (60 by 80 inches).

Futon folded for storing.

Futon lying flat.

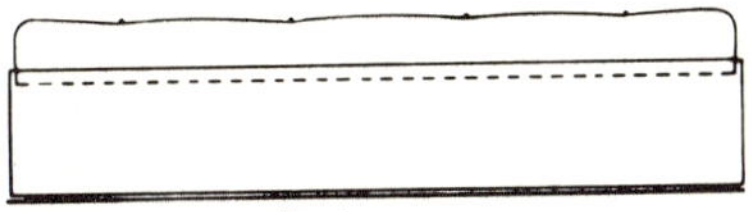

Futon on a platform.

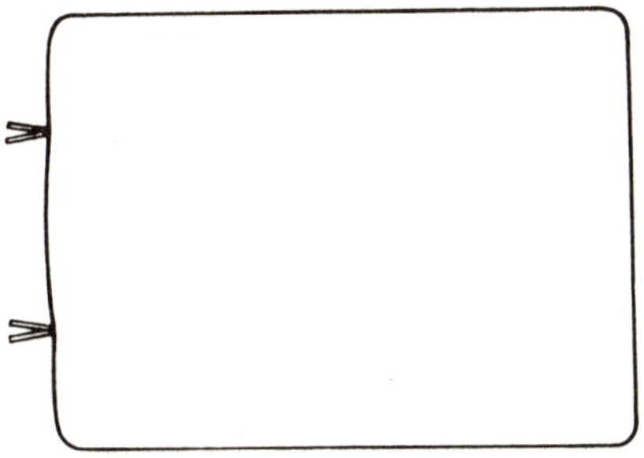

Futon cover with fabric ties on one end.

Two special muslin pillows from Shinera: above, a cylindrical one with a drawstring case; below, a small rectangular one. Both are filled with buckwheat hulls.

mattress, cannot be cleaned, the optional covers are convenient in protecting both the top and the bottom of the mattress. They can be machine washed and dried."

Special muslin pillows—small rectangular ones and cylindrical ones with drawstring cases—filled with buckwheat hulls are also available. Inquiries for information about these, futon covers, comforters, and ordering futons and maple bed frames with poplar slats should be directed to Shinera, P.O. Box 528, Boston, Mass. 02102.

Shinera has two retail outlets, one in Boston (at 229 Newbury Street) and one in New York (at 481 Columbus Avenue).

Joao Isabel's Brass Beds

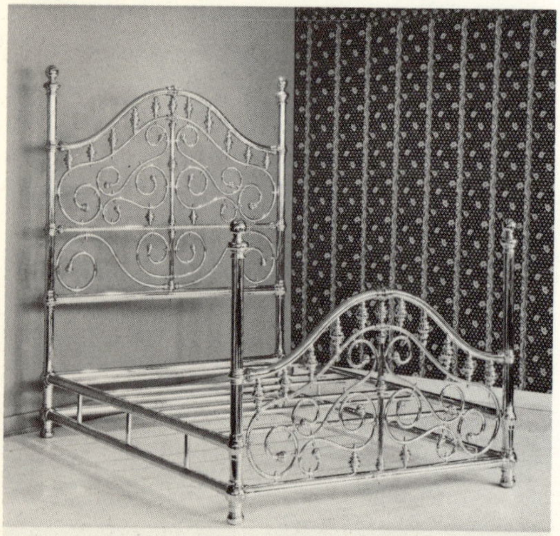

Few things are made today the way they were back in the good old days, and the brass beds made by Joao Isabel are no exception. But they are exceptional. The Portuguese-born Isabel and his partners and the craftsmen he employs have spent years (and considerable dollars) developing and perfecting techniques for constructing brass beds that have no comparable counterparts from any period, past or present. Besides the quality of workmanship that goes into building them, and the care that is taken in designing them, the most impressive difference between Joao Isabel's brass beds and just about anyone else's (old or new) is weight. All the fittings used to connect or terminate the heavy-gauge tubing (having walls .04 inch thick or thicker) in a typical Isabel brass bed are cast. Other brass-bed makers working today (with the exception of an occasional independent craftsman) use castings sometimes and stampings or "spinnings" at other times; but Joao Isabel uses castings all the time. There is only one stamping in the Isabel factory—the one used to show visitors the difference. "Castings," explains the Isabel catalog, "are structural or decorative pieces foundry-cast in solid metal. Stampings are purely decorative pieces formed from thin brass sheeting. To hear the difference between a casting and a stamping snap each piece with your fingernail. Better still, heft a casting in one hand and a stamping of the same size in the other. You'll feel the difference. Because of weakness, stampings have no structural value. And they may tear or dent as time passes. Castings are virtually indestructible. . . . We use foundry castings, exclusively, in the structure and decoration of all our headboards." A typically hefty Joao Isabel brass bed is the "Rosie" shown here; it weighs in at 230 pounds.

To make his beds even sounder, Isabel has developed a unique all-brass frame system that solidly connects the headboard to the footboard and also gives the bed a pleasing look of unity. Each of the frame's two-tube side rails fits snugly into cast-brass "T" joints in the head and foot; brass-headed bolts pass through the "T" joints and, screwing into

Top: *Joao Isabel's "Rosie."*

Center: *Joao Isabel's queen-size "Victoria."*

Bottom: *Joao Isabel's queen-size "Tulsa," with bedding removed to show the all-brass frame that connects the headboard to the footboard and supports the mattress and foundation.*

Detail of the "Tulsa" showing the "T" joint connections that couple the all-brass frame to the bed's headboard and footboard.

threaded steel elements in the ends of the tubular rails, secure the head and foot to the frame. Brass "slats" running from one side of the bed frame to the other provide support for a mattress and foundation.

Because of the amount of work and brass that goes into them, Joao Isabel beds aren't inexpensive. But compared with what a lot of other brass-bed makers offer for the same money or even a lot more, they're surprisingly reasonable.

Of the three beds pictured here, the "Tulsa" is the most expensive. In a queen-size (shown), the bed with headboard, footboard, and all-brass frame sells for $3,500, the headboard alone for $1,750, and the headboard and footboard with a specially designed steel frame connecting them for $2,900. The special steel frame for the headboard alone is available for an additional $35.

A Joao Isabel craftsman working on a nearly assembled "Porcelain Roundtop" headboard. The seven white balls near the top of the headboard are porcelain.

The 230-pound queen-size "Rosie" is $3,100 with headboard, footboard, and all-brass frame. The headboard alone is $1,400 ($35 more with a steel frame). The headboard/footboard/steel frame combination runs $2,500.

The "Victoria" in queen-size with headboard, footboard, and all-brass frame is $2,000. The headboard without the steel frame is $895; for the frame, add $35. $1,500 will get you the headboard, footboard, and steel frame between.

There are Joao Isabel brass bed models that are less ornate and less costly than the three shown here. A complete brass bed with headboard and footboard and steel frame can be yours for as little as $600. And $600 is what it would cost to put an all-brass frame between any Isabel headboard/footboard combination.

Joao Isabel has a showroom on Manhattan's East Side (at 120 East 32nd Street, New York, N.Y. 10016); a curvy neon sign at the entrance greets all visitors with a big, bright "Be Brassy." The Isabel factory is located across town (at 524 West 43rd Street), and visitors (by appointment) are also welcome there, to witness firsthand how Joao Isabel's heavy brass beds are handmade with a very unheavy hand. Three dollars will bring you the Joao Isabel catalog.

See also pages 90, 117, and 147.

Left: *A rough brass casting as it comes from the foundry. The short rod protruding from the top of the casting is called either a "tit" or a "nipple."*

Center: *The same casting after a number of turnings on a lathe. A craftsman called a fettler uses an assortment of chisellike tools to skillfully "scrape away" the rough surface of the casting, smoothing and shaping it as it spins.*

Right: *More turnings on the lathe followed by a series of polishings with increasingly finer abrasives finally turn the once-dull casting into a fine shiny finial weighing approximately three pounds. A brass stamping of similar size would weigh around four ounces.*

A Regency Headboard

Here is Regency Headboard A-26 "of finely carved mahogany, with ebony inlay," from Smith & Watson. Prices (headboard alone): single (or twin), $1,760; double, $2,210; dual (or king), $2,970. Made-to-order side and foot rails are available. See page 60.

The Emmentre Sleep Sofa

G. Faleschini's Emmetre Sleep Sofa is sold only to interior designers, decorators, and architects ("the trade"), and only by The Pace Collection Inc. (321 East 62nd Street, New York, N.Y. 10021). When its unique L-shaped cushions are removed, the Emmetre Sleep Sofa (no. 2003 in the Pace catalog) opens to a 55-inch-wide mattress. Its overall length when open is 88 inches. Closed, it measures 84 inches wide by 36 inches deep by 28 inches high. In Pace's "P" fabric, it goes for $2,650. Other fabrics are available, and other Pace showrooms are located in Chicago, Los Angeles, Miami, Boston, Dallas, San Francisco, and Seattle.

A Chippendale Lowpost Bedstead

"A fine and rare Chippendale mahogany lowpost bedstead. Philadelphia, c. 1760–1780. 6 feet 4 inches (1 m 93 cm) long, 52 inches (1 m 32 cm) wide," read the catalog description of this bed, which was auctioned off on March 10, 1978, at Christie's (Christie, Manson & Woods International Inc., 502 Park Avenue, New York, N.Y. 10022). It was something of a steal: the catalog estimated that it would go for somewhere between $6,000 and $8,000, and someone walked away with it for $4,400. See the reproduction on page 66.

Two details of the antique Chinese opium bed, showing the intricate mother-of-pearl inlay.

An Antique Chinese Opium Bed

The Chinese have been smoking in bed for centuries, presumably in beds like this one. It's an antique opium bed made of mahogany intricately inlaid with mother-of-pearl—an unbeatably exotic spot even for just sleeping. With a depth of 45 inches, 73 inches wide and 43½ inches high overall, its sleeping area is 38 inches by 68½ inches and rises 20½ inches off the floor. Knobkerry Third World Art & Design (158 Spring Street, New York, N.Y. 10012) is asking $8,500 for it, which hardly makes it an opium bed for the masses.

A queen-size reproduction Sheraton four-poster, model A-2.

A Reproduction Sheraton Four-Poster

The Smith & Watson catalog states:

"To make the finest furniture of the 20th century—this has always been our purpose and our aim. Since 1907 we have adhered to the highest principles of quality and design, making the name of Smith & Watson synonymous with the finest furniture made in this country or abroad.

"A cordial invitation is extended to visit our new showrooms at the Decorative Arts Center [in New York]. These larger quarters enable us to properly display our numerous new and old models. . . . We have an area set aside to exhibit the largest collection of fine headboards and high post beds in the world.

"Our expanded drafting department has increased our opportunity to work with the architects and interior designers in creating special furniture for the home and executive office. Designs from sketches are converted to working drawings, and then on to our cabinet shop where they are transformed into the desired piece. Having 25 of the most skilled

Detailed drawing from Smith & Watson's collection of hand-carved highpost beds and headboards.

European craftsmen, we are in the unique position of fulfilling every furniture need. In addition we have three cabinet shops in England and one on the Continent that produce furniture with meticulous care to detailed plans that we supply. These pieces are made of prepared woods, and constructed and finished by hand in the antique manner."

Smith & Watson headboards (see pages 55, 94, and 136) come in three stock sizes: single (or twin)—42 inches wide; queen—60 inches wide; and dual (or king)—80 inches wide. Other sizes are available by special order. Side and foot rails are made to order for all headboards. Prices are as follows: for single size, $330; for queen size, $480; and for dual (or king) size, $620.

While Smith & Watson's catalog is available to anyone who wants to buy one, their furniture is sold "to the trade only." For a copy of the catalog, send $4 to Smith & Watson, The Decorative Arts Center, 305 East 63rd Street, New York, N.Y. 10021.

The "Strips" Double Bed, Sofa Bed, Convertible Bed for Two

Below: *The "Strips" Sofa Bed, with its backrest flipped and bed coming unzipped.*

Bottom left: *The "Strips" Double Bed, zipped slightly open.*

Bottom right: *The "Strips" Sofa Bed, as a zipped-up sofa.*

One of the more interesting developments in furniture design during the 1970s was the appearance of a look that was fat, fluffy, and overstuffed. Some designers, Italy's Cini Boeri among them, took the look and incorporated it in modular units that could be arranged in numerous ways. Boeri's contribution was a plump collection called "Strips," and its manufacturer (Arflex of Milan) describes her creation this way:

"STRIPS are divided into three main groups: seat elements, modular elements, and beds with related headboards and side tables. Each unit consists of an expanded polyurethane foam structure of different densities over a wood base fitted with ABS plastic feet. Covers are quilted with polyester fiber filling. They are made of separate sections, held together by zippers, and attached to the base with snaps."

The "Strips" Double Bed is 186 cm (73¼ inches) wide, 221 cm (87 inches) long, and 42 cm (16½ inches) high. The bed is "opened up" by means of a zipper that runs around the top edge. The entire top cover may be zipped down, or only half: a zipper running down the middle of the top cover makes it possible to zip open one side of the bed only, while the other side remains shut. In the least expensive fabric, the "Strips" Double Bed is $2,540. A single bed, measuring 106 cm (41¾ inches) wide, goes for $1,525. Headboard and side table units are available for both.

The backrest of the "Strips" Sofa Bed flips back and its seat zips open to provide sleeping room for one. This flipping and zipping "Strips" unit is 213 cm (83⅞ inches) wide, 93 cm (36⅝ inches) deep, 63 cm (24¾ inches) high at the top of the backrest, and has a seat height of 40 cm (17¼ inches). Prices start at $1,905.

The backrest on the "Strips" Convertible Sofa for Two doesn't flip

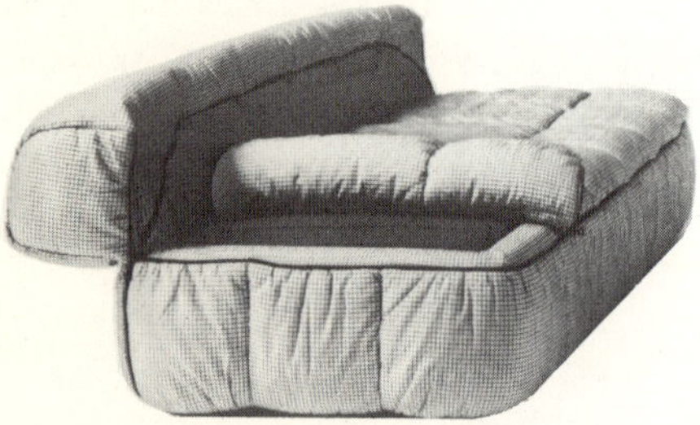

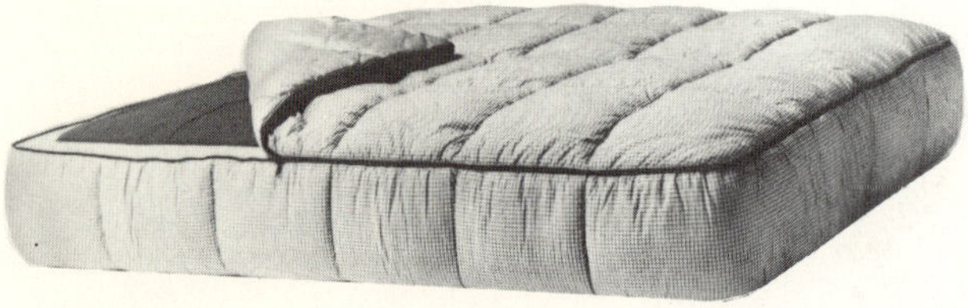

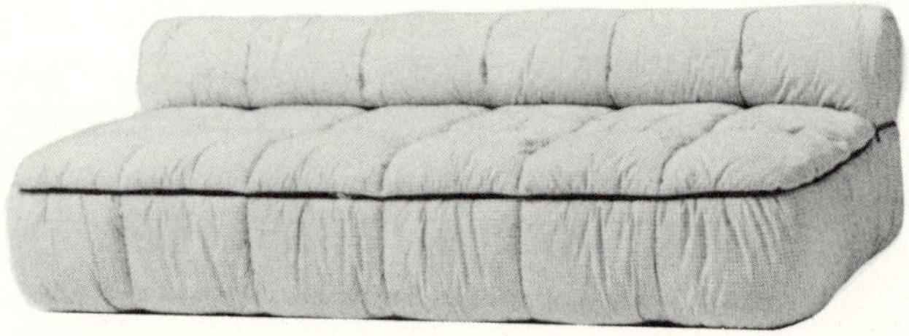

Left: *The "Strips" Convertible Sofa for Two, all dressed up and in the company of other "Strips" units.*

Right: *The "Strips" Double Bed, zipped open a little and surrounded at the head by a headboard unit and two side tables.*

Below: *A section from a catalog page showing the "Strips" Convertible Sofa for Two, closed and opened.*

back, but when its seat zips open a more or less conventional convertible sofa-type mattress frame flips out from inside. Zipped up, it measures 186 cm (73¼ inches) wide by 93 cm (36⅝ inches) deep by 63 cm (24¾ inches) high at the top of the backrest, and 44 cm (17¼ inches) high at the seat level. The "Strips" Convertible Sofa for Two can be yours (and, presumably, someone else's, too) for as little as $2,670.

The zippy, puffy "Strips" collection is imported into the United States and Canada by Beylerian, 305 East 63rd Street, New York, N.Y. 10021. Other Beylerian showrooms (open only to interior decorators, designers, and architects) are located in Chicago, Miami, Detroit, Los Angeles, San Francisco, and Seattle.

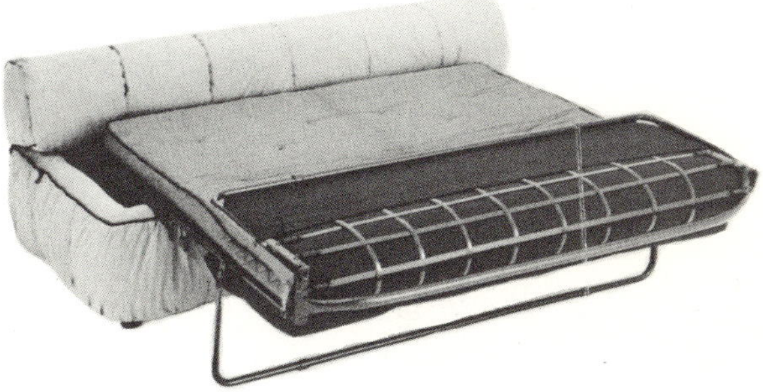

Colette's Beds

Top: *Colette in an installation called* Ancorra-tu *(from an Italian song title), "living in a space for six days with my personal belongings, objects and art works," at the Cologne Art Fair, October 25 to 31, 1977, in Cologne, Germany.*

Bottom: *Colette in her New York loft in 1978, posing as a "doll" in front of one of her ever-changing at-home bed environments.*

Colette, a highly regarded New York artist, is often publicly observed sleeping on the job, for the conceptual environments that are her art almost always include a bed, and the bed invariably includes Colette—sound asleep or merely lounging, surrounded by personal possessions, tape recorders playing or televisions televising, small works of art, photographic images, and other meaningful objects. In creating her surreal, cocoonlike sleeping spaces she employs seemingly endless yards of satin, veiling, parachute silk, and similarly sensuous material, gathering it, bunching it up and tacking it down, draping it and allowing it to cascade diaphanously above, around, and over the bed. Well-placed backlighting heightens the effect.

Colette has installed bed environments—with such titles as *Persephone's Bedroom, The Wake of Madame Recamier, In Memory of Ophelia and All Those Who Have Died of Love and Madness*, and *If It Takes Forever, I Will Wait for You*—in galleries and museums both in Europe and in the United States, including the Museum of Modern Art in New York. Her own living and working space, a loft in Manhattan's SoHo district, is a constantly evolving environment with an ever-changing bed setting as the center of interest.

But you don't have to go to a gallery or museum to see a genuine Colette bed environment. You can have one of your very own. For a price, she will gladly take suitable quantities of suitably filmy, shiny, and drapable material, lights, your own cherished objects and photographs, audio and/or video tape equipment, and mirrors, and use them to transform your existing bed (or one supplied by her for the occasion) into a work of art, one that can have *you* as the human element "performing" inside.

It can be a "limited" environment, involving only the bed and a small surrounding structure, or a total floor-to-ceiling transformation of an entire room. The price of the former, according to the artist, would start at around $9,000; the latter, at around $20,000. Art, like life, isn't cheap.

Colette's service number is 212-825-0482.

Opposite: *Colette in* "Let Them Eat Cake" (Marie Antoinette au Petit Trianon), *an installation and performance with audio at the Paris Biennale, October 1977.*

This American lowpost Chippendale bed reproduction from the Douglas Campbell Company is 38 inches high at the highest point and 18 inches high at the rails. It can be ordered in mahogany or walnut, and either will be stained to order. A single or double bed is $655, a queen is $675, and a king is $695. See page 114. See also the bed that was sold at auction on page 57.

A Reproduction Chippendale Lowpost Bedstead

An American Red Oak Bed

A close look at some fine late-19th-century carving.

Standing in front of In Days of Old, Ltd. (357 Atlantic Avenue, Brooklyn, N.Y. 11217), is a very fine American red oak bed from just before the turn of the century. What makes it so fine is the nature of its carvings; the decorative work at the top of the headboard and footboard is incised directly into the wood, as opposed to being applied in sections, the method commonly employed on "mass-produced" furniture of the same period. Considering the quality of the work involved, the $750 price tag on the bed doesn't seem at all excessive. In Days of Old, Ltd., specializes in higher-quality old oak furniture and usually has a good assortment of exceptional beds.

The "Unodue" Bed

"The Unodue Bed," says The Pace Collection Inc., importer of the S. T. Mariani/G. Faleschini–designed bed, "is defined by a channeled, upholstered headboard and bed frame. The bed comes complete with a pair of fully upholstered two-drawer night tables with solar bronze glass tops, matching bedspread and pillow shams, as well as a mattress. The Unodue Bed is a luxurious focal point for the fashionable bedroom."

The bed size is 81 inches wide by 91 inches long by 30½ inches high. The mattress measures 63 inches wide by 75 inches long by 7 inches high. It can be had from Pace only through an interior decorator, designer, or architect, for $4,350 in what Pace calls its "P" fabric.

The "Togo" Bed

Designed in France (by Michel Ducaroy for a company called Roset), manufactured in Canada (by Arconas/Airborne Corp., Toronto), and sold in most major cities in the United States and Canada is a bed called "Togo." According to the Arconas/Airborne catalog: "Togo Bed includes a queen-size urethane mattress 4 inches thick on an all-foam support base. Quilt-bedspread combination is held down by Velcro around bottom edge. Quilted cover on head end is removable for dry cleaning. Togo Bed can be supplied without mattress for customer's own mattress not exceeding 5-inch thickness." The bed's overall dimensions are 92 inches long by 64 inches wide by 15 inches high (at the mattress level) by 30 inches high (at the top of the "headboard"). The sleeping area measures 64 by 78 inches. Prices range from approximately $1,600 (when covered in the most humble fabric) to around $3,900 (covered in a top-grade leather). To get a "Togo" you have to go to someone in "the trade"—an interior designer, decorator, or architect. One of them can get it from Arconas/Airborne, whose New York showroom is at 150 East 58th Street, New York, N.Y. 10022.

A Handed-Down Maple Bed

This bed didn't cost its owner anything. It's a hand-me-down—a strikingly simple early 20th-century maple bed that Richard Barlow, a collector of chairs, tables, lamps, art pottery, and other items generated by the American Arts and Crafts Movement (see page 144), acquired from his parents; they bought it during the 1930s in Virginia. The chair next to the headboard is a signed Gustav Stickley. The bed, whose maker and date are unknown, stands out in the open in one corner of its owner's large loft space in New York's SoHo district.

Perhaps there's a bed somewhere that won't cost you anything. Have you checked lately to see if someone in your family has an interesting bed he might want to hand down to you?

Trundle Bed Plans to Send For

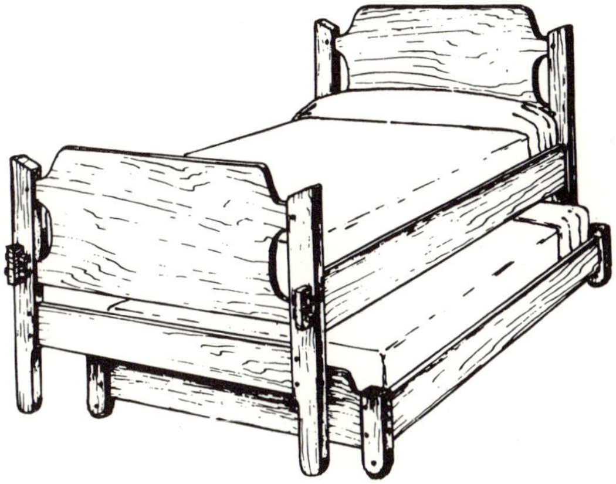

Here's a trundle bed you can make from full-sized plans from Furniture Designs (1425 Sherman Avenue, Evanston, Ill. 60201). Their catalog of plans describes it this way: "Here is an unusual item. The word 'trundle' means a small wheel, and that is exactly what the lower bed has—small wheels made of wood. It is ideal for use in a child's room since it is such a space-saver. The joinery is accomplished with keyed and pegged tenons as used by early craftsmen. The overall height is 39½ inches."

Send $7 to Furniture Designs, ask for plan 165, and the trundle bed plan will be sent to you. For more information about Furniture Designs plans, see page 108. See also page 48.

More Trundle Bed Plans to Send For

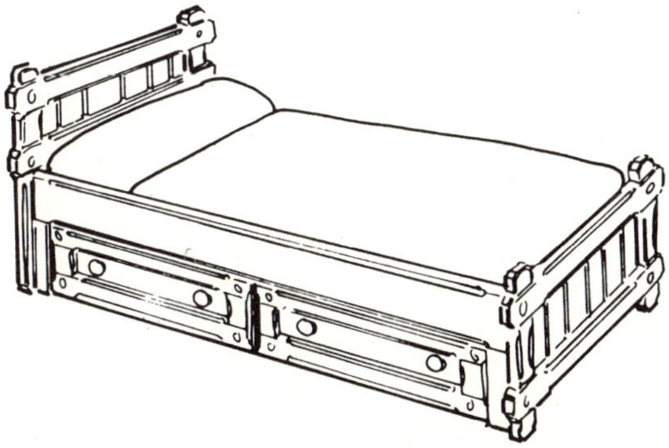

Carter Woodkit (P.O. Box 156, Bridgewater, Conn. 06752), seller of the plans for the bed illustrated here, explains that all their plans "are geared to the home craftsman. Simple shop equipment and basic woodworking knowledge is all you need. . . . Patterns and shapes can be traced directly from the print to material. The plans come with bill of materials and a perspective drawing showing assembly. Hardware and supply sources are noted."

All of Carter Woodkit's plans are available in "Early American, Spanish, or Modern America look." The bed shown here (Plan 443) is the Modern America trundle bed. The Spanish trundle bed is Plan 343, and the Early American trundle bed is Plan 243. Each is $10.50.

A Roll-Top Bed

Roll-top desks by the thousands rolled off early 20th-century furniture makers' assembly lines, and roll-tops have recently rolled up popular support once again. But the idea of putting roll-top technology and beds together doesn't seem to have rolled around in anyone's head until Scottish designer Angus J. Bruce rolled out of his shop a custom-built contemporary mahogany bed with sliding tambour doors in the headboard.

The doors in Bruce's original roll-top bed (shown) roll down to permit lamps to extend from inside. And then there are nonrolling doors in the side of the bed—one that pops straight up and snaps into place as a table, and another that opens on hinges to allow access to storage space inside.

Another Angus J. Bruce roll-top bed design (also shown) features a roll-top door in the foot that conceals a pop-up TV. Both beds are built with solid mahogany and mahogany veneer and measure overall approximately 102 inches long, 80 inches wide, and 36 inches high. To buy one, you need a roll containing $5,500. Delivery, says Angus (398 West Broadway, New York, N.Y. 10012), should take ten to twelve weeks.

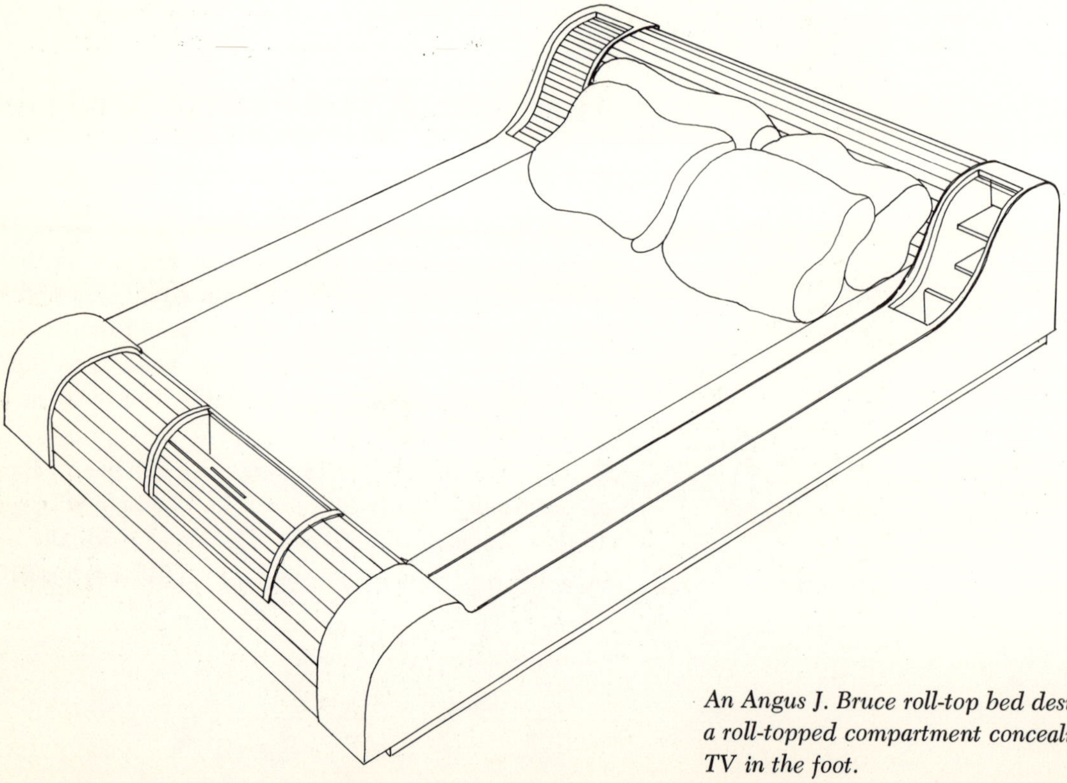

An Angus J. Bruce roll-top bed design featuring a roll-topped compartment concealing a pop-up TV in the foot.

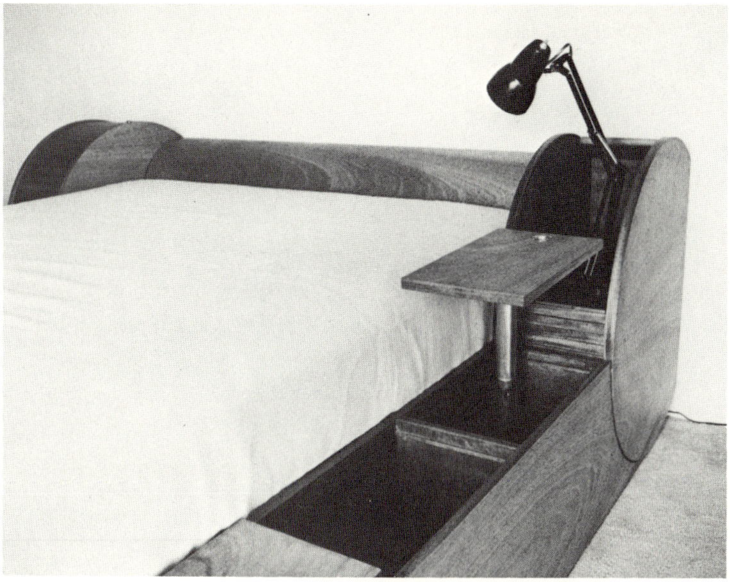

Detail of Angus J. Bruce's roll-top bed showing its roll-top door rolled down, its lamp extended, and its side doors popped up and flipped back.

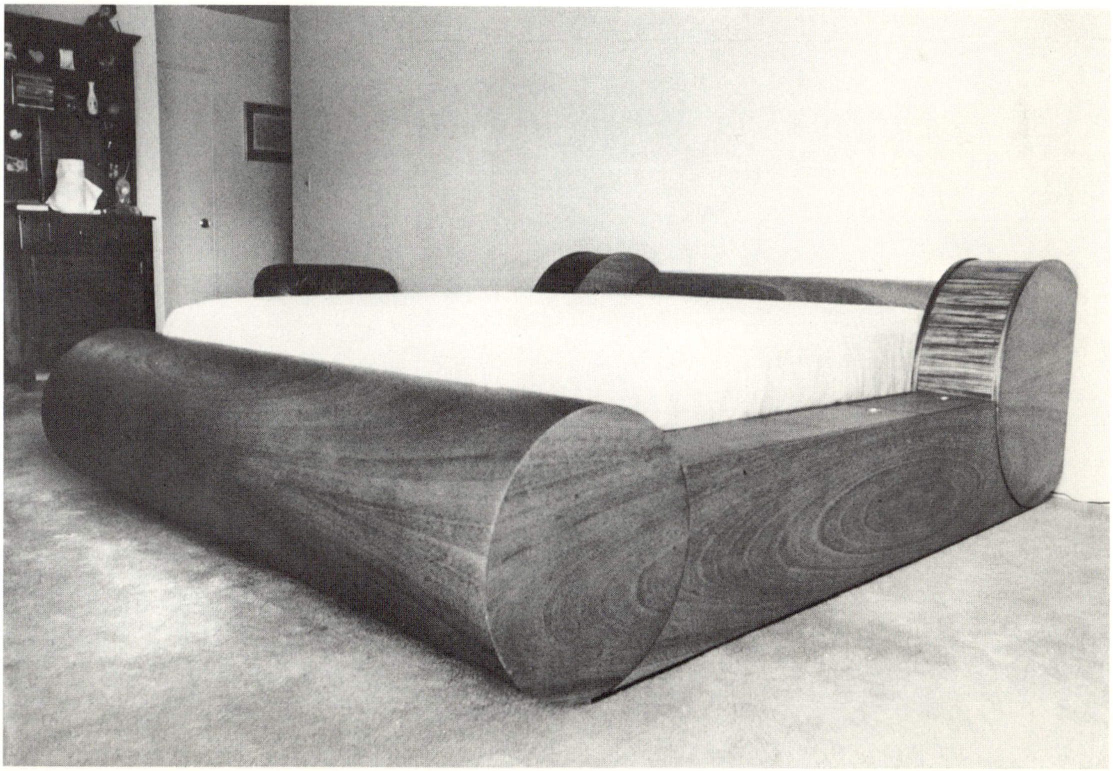

Marcello Mioni's Brass Bed

This very different, very modern, very low-profile-for-a-brass-bed brass bed's posts call to mind a whole variety of similarly shaped objects, from bullets to lipsticks.

Designed by Marcello Mioni of Rome/Los Angeles, it comes in either queen or king sizes, is sold to the public only through interior designers, decorators, and architects, and costs $5,775. This bed is no. 470 in their catalog, which you may send away for to the U.S. Marcello Mioni showroom at 114 North Robertson Boulevard, Los Angeles, Calif. 90048.

In a mythological tale told by the Roman poet Ovid, the nymph Daphne escaped from the persistent advances of a lovesick Apollo by getting herself turned into a tree. Apollo then fell madly in love with the tree. More than a decade ago, woodworker Tommy Simpson made a bed with four highly abstracted Daphnes that have turned into bed posts holding up a leaf-green canopy. Made of pine and butternut wood and appropriately called "Daphne," it was one of the featured attractions in a 1966 exhibition entitled "The Bed," held at New York's Museum of Contemporary Crafts. It is presently in storage and still very much for sale. The artist is asking $2,500 for it, which isn't really a lot, especially not if you happen to fall in love with any or all of the posts.

For more information, contact Tommy Simpson, 123 Byram Shore Road, Greenwich, Conn. 06830.

Tommy Simpson's "Daphne" Canopy Bed

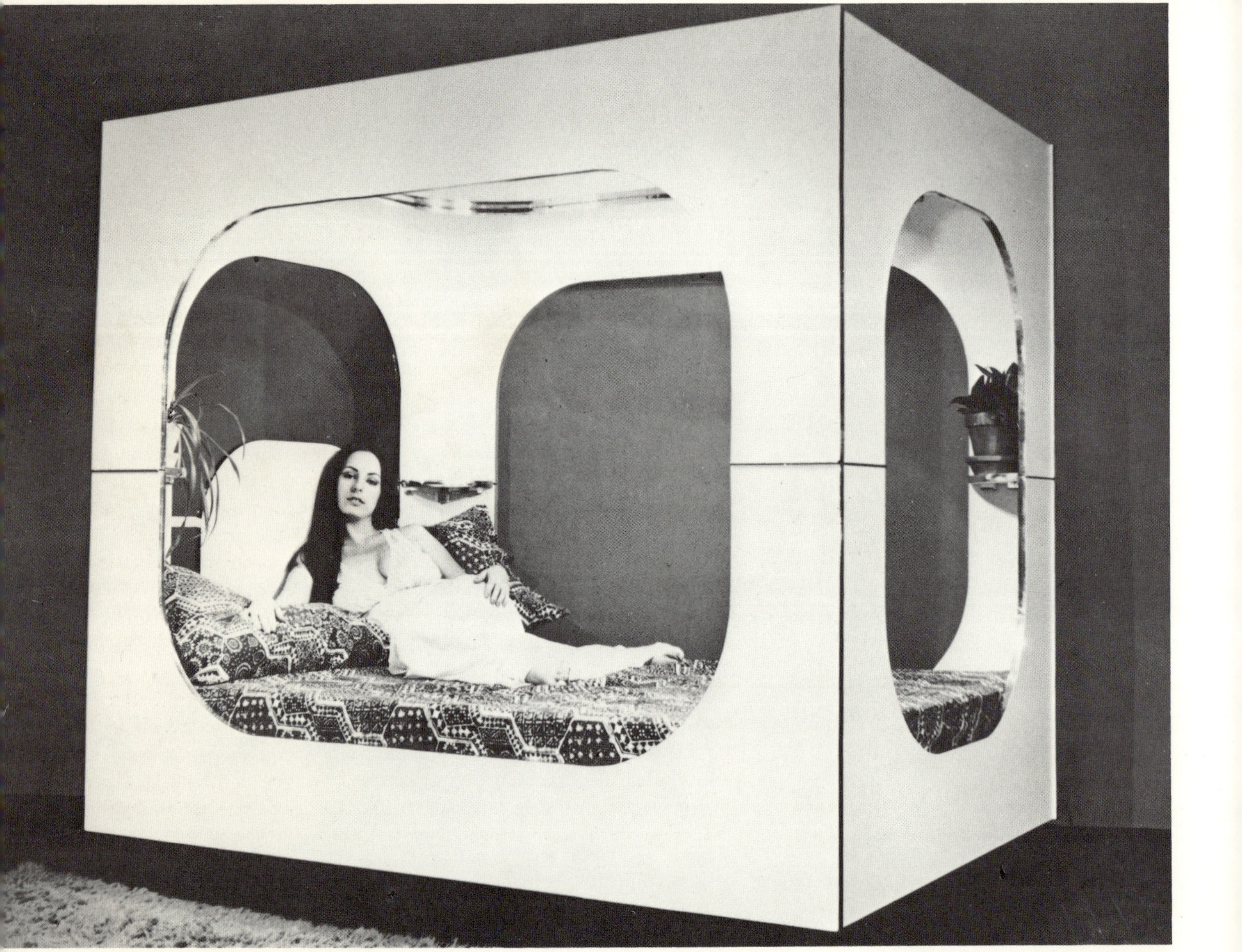

The Sleep Box® by Loftcraft

Randy Parsons, owner of Loftcraft and designer of its furniture, describes his company's premier product, The Sleep Box®, and why he designed it:

"I consider a designer to be a servant to the public essentially. He solves their problems with spaces, and lends a trained eye for aesthetics. Most of my furniture is designed to solve problems in room space (loft beds, platform beds, wall units) but with The Sleep Box® I wanted to solve a different kind of space problem. A friend told me that with two kids, a dog, and a cat, he and his wife didn't really have a space of their own, even though they lived in a large West Side [of New York City] apartment. So I designed The Sleep Box® to solve a problem in space on an emotional level. Even though it's a very open bed, it tends to cut off a kind of psychological noise and permit one to relax. It's a very romantic bed, designed purely for fun. Not surprisingly, two years after its introduction, we called several hundred Sleep Box® owners to find who they were. We discovered that forty-seven percent are married, most with children, and another forty-two percent are living with someone in a serious relationship. I'm glad to see it works."

Like other items of Loftcraft furniture (see pages 103 and 148), The Sleep Box® arrives disassembled in a box. Putting it together, Loftcraft assures, is both easy and fun. Sleep Boxes come in white (as shown), black, oak, rosewood, or walnut. Optional reading lights, clock radio, speakers, stained glass panels, and Mirrex (a type of plastic) ceiling mirror are also available. Loftcraft will send all kinds of additional information and prices to anyone requesting them. They're at 171 Seventh Avenue, New York, N.Y. 10011.

There is a very fine woodworking magazine called, appropriately, *Fine Woodworking*, and it is the undisputed bible of people who take their work with wood seriously. Each of the magazine's issues contains shoptalk that encompasses every conceivable aspect of the cabinetmaker's discipline, but only rarely does what one would call a "how-to" article appear. An article called "Hidden Beds: Two Ways to Get More Sleeping Space," by David Landen, was one of those exceptions. It appeared in the Fall 1976 issue and featured two exceptional beds: a handsome settle bed and a couch with a sliding seat that transforms it into a bed. That article is reprinted in its entirety here with the kind permission of Taunton Press, publisher of *Fine Woodworking*. An experienced woodworker would have no trouble following the plans given.

Fine Woodworking is published quarterly (in March, June, September, and December). A one-year subscription (in the United States) is $12, $22 for two years. Back issues (starting with the Winter 1975 issue) are available. The address of Taunton Press is P.O. Box 355, Newtown, Conn. 06470.

Hidden Beds: Two Ways to Get More Sleeping Space

From *Fine Woodworking* magazine:

"Beds for which there is little space or which are used only occasionally pose interesting problems for a furnituremaker. They should not only be comfortable to sleep on and take up a minimum of space when not in

Author used mostly 8/4 stock for the couch because it was readily available. Drawing (page 80) gives general dimensions and an idea of how it was put together. Owners use a foam rubber mattress for sleeping rather than the cushions shown.

use, but also should work reasonably well as another piece of furniture. Of the two pieces discussed in this article, the couch works better as another piece of furniture while the settle, with its full-sized mattress already made up, is the most useful as a bed.

"Neither one is a particularly original design (couches with sliding seats probably originated in Denmark or Sweden, and settles have been around for a long time), but each had to be worked out to fit a client's specifications. The couch was made of red oak and the settle of cherry. Almost any strong hardwood will work for the couch and the settle could be made from almost anything, including plywood for the carcase. Cherry was used because of the client's preference and because eight-foot sections of clear stock in reasonable widths are still available.

"*The Couch.* Overall dimensions are not critical. It must be long enough for someone to lie on, and the seat deep and high enough to be comfortable. The depth of the seat determines to some extent the width of the slide-out bed. In this couch, the extended width is something over 40 inches, which is wide enough for two people to sleep on occasionally. Aligning the slats in the back of the couch with the stationary slats in the seat would have made it possible to extend the sliding slats through the back and thus gain several inches of bed width. But this wasn't done because it would have kept the couch out too far from the wall or would have made it unsightly when positioned with the back exposed.

"Construction of the couch is relatively straightforward once the

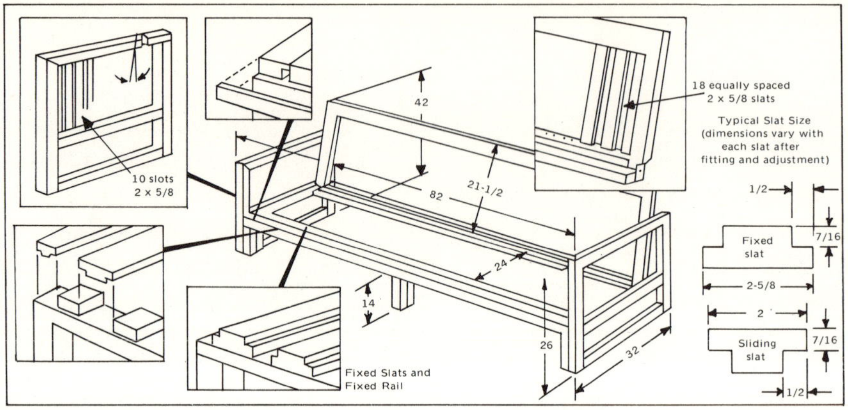

basic dimensions are determined and a layout sheet drawn up. I used 8/4 stock for the frame. The two end pieces and the back are joined with open mortise and tenon joints. The end cross pieces and the slats are mortised into the frame. A dado about 1/2-inch deep cut into the inside of the top piece of the end frame at the appropriate angle for the slant of the back and a rabbet the same depth and corresponding angle at the bottom end of the vertical piece on the back hold the back and ends together. The front rail rests on two legs glued to the end pieces. A third leg is added in the center.

"Slats milled from 4/4 stock, with a rabbet cut on each side, cut square on the front end and beveled to match the angle of the back on the back end, are spaced evenly and screwed and glued to the top side of the front rail and to a cleat fastened to the bottom piece of the back. The sliding part of the seat consists of three legs supporting a front rail into which has been cut a series of dadoes to hold the sliding slats which are first fastened with screws to allow for adjusting the fit, and later marked and glued. These slats can be left a little short of the edge of the front rail and a facing strip attached later to cover the end grain and the gap left by the rabbets.

"Because the large number of pieces compounds any tendency to bind, about 1/4-inch of play per slat was initially allowed, and the rough spots later cleaned up. I briefly considered tongue and groove slats for the sliding mechanism. They are probably esthetically superior, but less likely to maintain a flat surface for the seat, difficult to fit and nearly impossible to keep working smoothly.

"*The Settle.* Dimensions were determined from the size of the mattress and the room into which the piece has to fit. The mattress should be measured for length, width, thickness, and the amount of compression which results when one sits on the edge. After some allowance has been made for bedding, these measurements are used to lay out the box which holds the mattress. The sides of the box were cut from 6/4 stock and dovetailed together. Dovetails are somewhat awkward to cut on long pieces, but, if done accurately, they prevent winding and make assembly much easier.

"To support the mattress, strips about 1¼ × 1 inch were glued to the inside of the box on all four sides. A center strip, with ½-inch rabbets on each side and ½-inch thicker than the side strips are wide (so the top of the strip will be flush with the plywood bottom set into the rabbets), was set into dadoes cut into the strips around the inside edge. The strips supporting the plywood bottom should all stop about an inch short of the bottom of the box in the same plane so a support for the center arm can be added later and so the foot can support the entire bottom of the bed, not just the two sides.

"Because they form the back of the settle when the bed is raised, the two pieces of plywood are placed good face down in the box. They should be selected for color and figure match with the wood in the settle and the plywood for the back of the carcase. One-half-inch plywood is probably the thinnest one can use for the bottom. Three-quarter-inch would be more secure, but it makes the bed rather heavy to lift up and down, particularly if the mattress is anything other than a light foam rubber.

"Once the box is complete, the layout for the rest of the piece can be drawn up. The width of the bed plus an inch or so clearance becomes the inside dimension of the carcase. Both the height and the depth of the carcase are determined by the location of the pivot point. Perhaps the easiest method for working out this detail is to make a cardboard cutout the same size and shape as the side of the bed with the mattress in place and to use a pin as an easily movable pivot. Assuming one centers the pivot in the side of the bed, trial and error shows that as the pivot moves toward the foot of the bed, the carcase becomes deeper and shorter, and that, if the bottom of the bed rests on the seat, the distance the center of the pivot is above the seat has to equal the distance the pivot is behind the seat. The seating height, plus one-half the width of the bed side, plus the distance from the pivot center to the top corner of the bed or the top corner of the mattress, whichever is greater, becomes the minimum inside height of the carcase. The seating depth, plus one-half the width of the bed side plus the distance from the pivot center to the top corner of the head of the bed or the top corner of the mattress, becomes the minimum inside depth of the carcase interior. The overall dimension of the carcase should be checked against the dimensions of the room into which the settle is to go to make sure it will fit through the doorway and can be tipped upright once inside.

"When the layout has been drawn up from these dimensions, the carcase sides are glued up from 4/4 stock, the profile cut, and the top and sides dovetailed. Again, the dovetails are hard to cut, but well worth the trouble saved during assembly. The seat, which gets put together at this time, is simply a box with a hinged lid. The front and back of the box are set into slots cut in the carcase sides and reinforced with glue blocks and screws, and the bottom set into rabbets cut in the front and back of the box and supported on the ends by cleats attached to the carcase with screws in slotted holes. The front of the box should be set back one-half to three-quarters of an inch from the front edge of the carcase to allow for overhang of the hinged seat lid. Attached to the top of the back piece of the box is a piece of 8/4 stock with a rabbet the thickness of the seat lid cut in the top front. This piece will support the seat when the hinges begin to sag, which they inevitably do.

"After the carcase has been assembled and the seat fixed in place, rabbets can be cut to receive the carcase back. In this case, three pieces of ½-inch plywood were used, each being separated by a strip similar to the one used down the center of the bottom of the bed. Three pieces help break up the space and also yield better cuts from 4 × 8 sheets. The dividing strips are fastened into the rabbet at the top of the carcase and into a rabbet cut in a cross piece installed near the bottom of the back of the carcase.

General dimensions and some details of settle are shown in drawing (page 85). Those wishing to make their own should first design around the mattress they get and the room it will be in. In photos, removable legs can barely be seen stored under the closed settle.

"Once the carcase has been squared up with the back, it should be carefully leveled in every direction, using shims, clamps, props, or whatever is necessary, because pieces this size tend to shift alignment whenever they are moved or rest on an uneven surface, even though every effort is made to avoid winding and lopsidedness during assembly. After leveling, the seat lid can be mounted on the hinges. Remember to keep them far enough away from the sides of the carcase to avoid being hit by the descending bed. The seat is cut into two pieces three or four inches off center so that the box can be gotten into without removing the center arm rest.

"While the carcase is still level and the seat lids are in place, the bed can be tried in the open position to check for alignment of the pivot points. If these have been carefully laid out on both the carcase and the bed, 1/16-inch holes drilled through the carcase and partway into the bed should line up when a piece of stiff wire is stuck through the carcase hole. With the bed resting squarely on the seat, there shouldn't be much trouble in readjusting the pivot point one way or another to allow the bed to close squarely. Once the alignment is as close as possible, holes about 2 inches in diameter can be drilled through the carcase and through the sides of the bed. Pins about 8 inches long were turned with a slight taper so they could be driven tightly into the inside of the bed frame and still turn freely in the same sized hole in the carcase. The pivot pins can be fastened with wedges or some other device, but whatever is used should permit easy disassembly since the carcase is heavy to move around even without the bed. With the bed raised and clamped in the closed position, two more holes drilled through the carcase and partway into the bed frame about 5 feet above the floor and fitted with turned pins will hold the bed in place when it is not being used.

"The center arm rest is mounted onto the center strip of the bottom of the bed. A slot dovetail was cut into a piece of stock the same width as the center strip and the same thickness as the distance between the strip and the bottom of the bed frame (it rests on the seat and helps support the bottom of the bed). A corresponding pin on the edge of a board supporting the arm fits into the dovetail slot snugly and permits the arm to rest squarely on the slotted piece and tightly against the center strip. The pinned piece can be removed easily to let the bed come down.

"The legs to support the foot of the bed are joined together with a crosspiece using open mortise and tenon joints. The leg assembly is a separate, detached piece, trimmed for a friction fit inside the bed frame against the strips holding the plywood bottom. The cross piece at the top supports the plywood bottom in the center where it is the weakest, and it does this especially well if the legs are positioned 12 to 16 inches from the end of the bed when it is let down. The legs are stored under the seat when not in use.

"The seats in both the settle and the couch are completely horizontal rather than sloped slightly toward the back. In the couch, cushions help alleviate this comfort problem somewhat. But in the settle, the problem is compounded by the back not being slanted either. Cushions on the seat or on the back might help. The deeper than usual seat helps some as does the tendency to sit in the corners.

"The variations possible with either of these designs are amost unlimited. With the couch, any sort of end piece and back design is possible, and the slats for the seat could be replaced with two pieces of plywood, or possibly three to make that seat slide out to full double-bed size. With the settle, changes in the profile of the sides, edge treatment, facing strips and so on can change its appearance considerably. One could even eliminate the carcase and mount the bed in a hole cut in a wall."

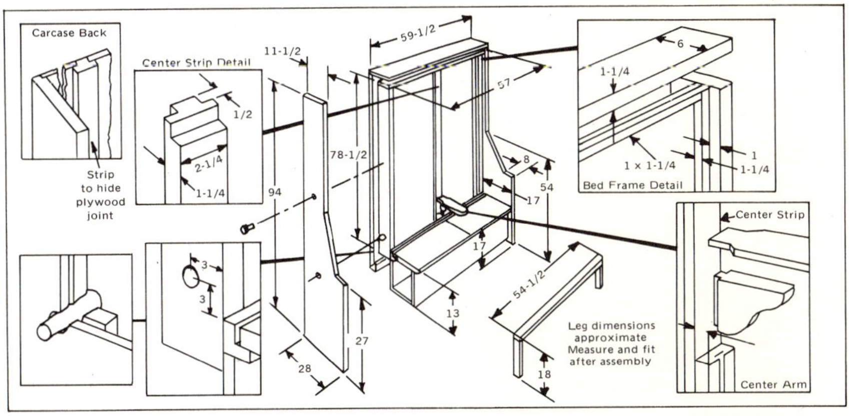

Bruno Munari's "Abitacolo" Bed

"Che cos'è un ABITACOLO*?" "Was ist ein* ABITACOLO*?" "Qu'est-ce qu'un* ABITACOLO*?"* A brochure explaining Bruno Munari's deservedly famous children's bed structure asks and answers that question in four different languages. In English it goes like this:

"What's an ABITACOLO? It's the Italian word for 'cockpit,' the enclosed space for the pilot in a small plane or a boat. But the Italians also use ABITACOLO for a car's interior, or for a spaceship's crew compartment. In short, ABITACOLO is 'habitable space' in its essential form. Figuratively, it's an individual's intimate recess, the place that encloses a man's own little world.

"In the home—built by adults for adults—not always has a boy an

Bruno Munari's "Abitacolo" bed, manufactured by Robots (Milan, Italy) and sold in the United States by Ambienti.

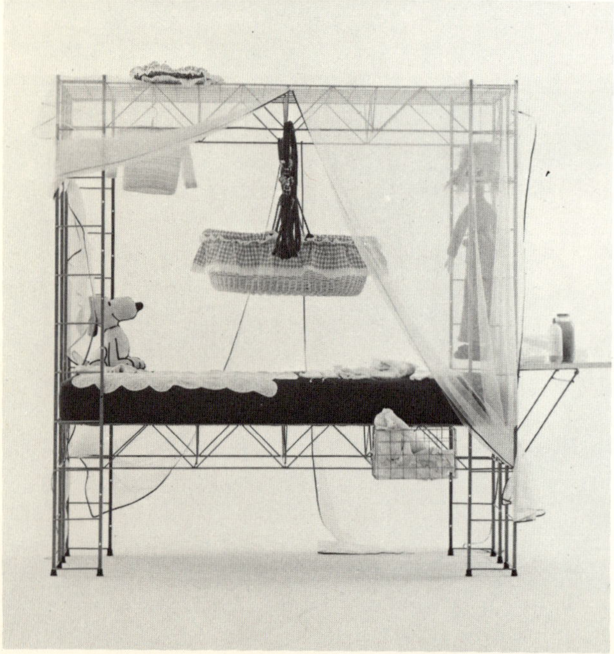

ABITACOLO all to himself. Only the luckiest kids have their own room—a room they can furnish and transform as they like. Generally, all they have is a bed, a table, a chair, a shelf for their books, oftentimes no more than a suitcase for clothes. They have no nook, no ABITACOLO where they may isolate themselves, where they may study, write, read, sleep, listen to the music they love, chat with their friends—or just think.

"This is the state of things that ABITACOLO was originated from—as an attempt to solve the problem from the structural as well as from the 'appearance' standpoint—and in terms of cost, too . . . which [is] by no means less important.

"ABITACOLO is a steel structure reduced to its very essence. Its module is 20 centimeters (approx. 8 inches) and, with all its sub-multiples, it ensures the highest all-around flexibility in assembly. It's a welded steel structure covered with epoxy resins baked on at a temperature of 400°F. The color is a very pale gray. The base structure incorporates a tilting, adjustable-height table. Two 80 × 190-cm (32 × 76-inch) panels can be installed on the four uprights. Their height may be chosen at will, and the uprights double as ladders. Erection is so simple that no instructions are supplied. All one has to do is tighten 8 wingnuts.

"Two catch-all metal baskets may be hooked just where they are needed. And some 20 hooks are available, too—for hanging practically anything anywhere. The whole thing weighs just 51 kg—or approx. 110 lbs.

"Once erected, the structure will be as solid as if welded. Let Mr. Overweight try it. No matter how fat, he won't be able to smash the thing. No matter how hard he tries. In fact, tests have proven that ABITACOLO can support as many as 20 people.

"ABITACOLO is entirely neutral in appearance. In other words, it 'goes' with practically any interior decoration scheme. It imposes no aesthetics of its own—just because it's an 'essential' structure. In fact, it lends itself to any alteration or transformation. Indeed, the more intrusive its user, the less conspicuous it becomes."

If that explanation doesn't answer your every question, or if you want more information about shipping and price, contact Ambienti, 792 Madison Avenue, New York, N.Y. 10021. The last time it was checked, the price was $610.

The "DS-76"

Turner Ltd. (305 East 63rd Street, New York, N.Y. 10021) imports the DS-76 system, designed by De Sede of Switzerland, and describes it this way: "An informal suite for easy-going young moderns with lots of friends. The DS-76 seating elements are extra wide: they can be used individually and each can be easily converted into a comfortable bed. The upholstery is double-seamed. The upper part of the upholstery consists of the proven Bultex-foam combination and a cushion filled with new, down-like synthetic fibers. It rests on a sub-upholstery supported by a wooden frame and rubber straps covered by a Bultex-foam layer. Sleeping area measures 225 cm (88.5 in.) × 90 cm (35.4 in.)."

Turner will sell the DS-76 elements only to "the trade": interior decorators, designers, and architects. Any of these can obtain the single armless element shown at a cost to you of $1,200 in canvas and either $1,589 or $1,884 in leather, depending on the grade.

An arrangement of DS-76 elements. Each element turns into a bed, which could make for some interesting possibilities should a large party get out of hand.

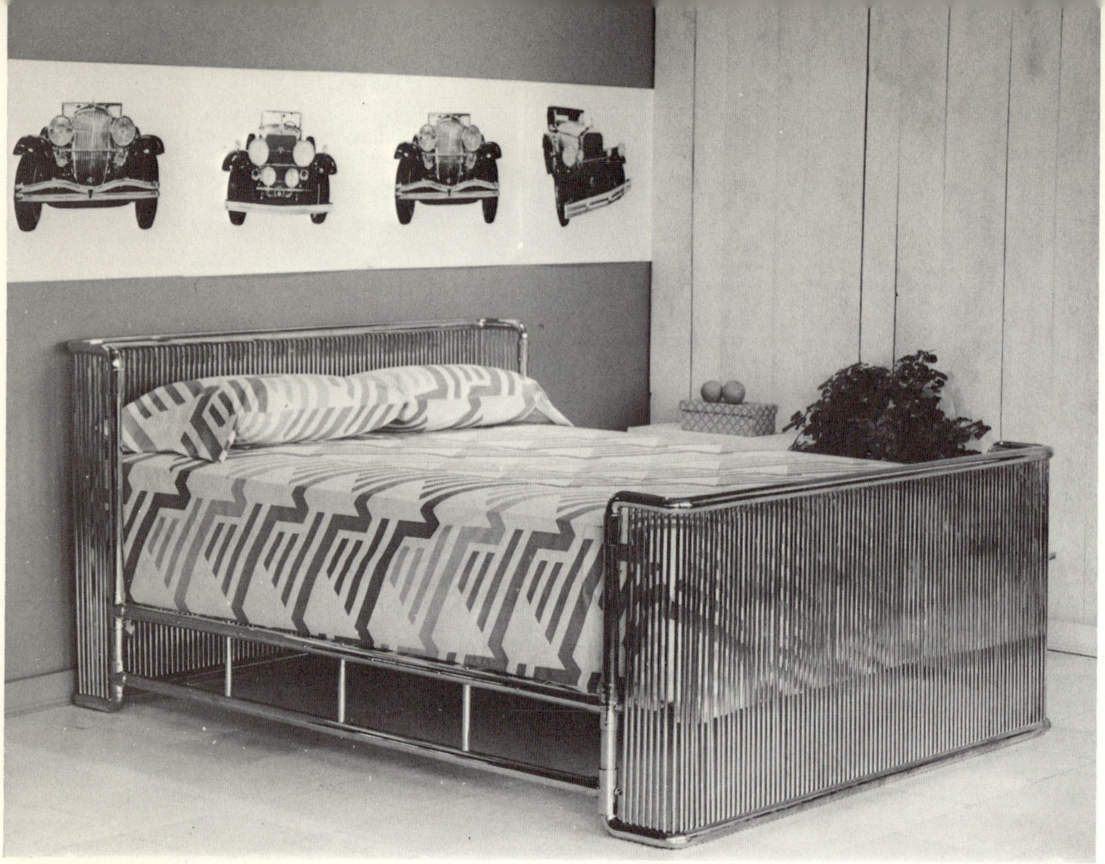

Joao Isabel's "California" Brass Bed

Brass-bed maker Joao Isabel's "California" is a strikingly contemporary custom design developed for a customer in California. Scores of sketches were made as the design slowly evolved. Countless hours were spent planning and working out the construction details. New methods of assembly had to be devised. And yet, the price the customer was charged was only $4,500, because Isabel retained the right to make the bed for anyone else who might want one—for the same price, of course. So he doesn't charge a custom customer for all the extra time and effort that goes into developing and producing a custom design. (Had the California customer wanted his bed to remain one of a kind, the price would have been several times higher.)

A custom-made Joao Isabel brass bed needn't run you $4,500 either. A fairly simple yet unique design could be ordered for considerably less. How much less? Ask Joao Isabel. His showroom is at 120 East 32nd Street, New York, N.Y. 10016. (See page 52.)

Harvard's "Super Stackers"

Question: When is a Harvard dorm bed not a bed from a Harvard dormitory? Answer: When it's a dormitory bed made by the Harvard Manufacturing Company, the people who brought you the ubiquitous Harvard bed frame. A very minimal Harvard dorm bed that's guaranteed to take a licking and keep on supporting mattress and ticking is Harvard's "Super Stacker." "Harvard's newest, strongest, best-looking dorm beds" are, in the words of the manufacturer, "more rigid than conventional stacking beds. Hefty 1¼-inch square steel tube ends, and hook-in end-support construction. Easily assembled. Changes quickly from a 'sleeps 2' stacker into single dorm beds, and back again. No tools required. No extra stacking parts to buy. Use it 3 ways: as a complete stacker, a single bed, or 'base only' plus loose hook plates to attach to your own headboards. Factory installed headboards available . . . walnut finish, laminated on both sides, ¾ inch thick. Super Stackers feature Spiro-Spring construction, concealed double earlock hooks at corners, 2 × 1½-inch steel angle bases, round tubular spreader bars."

Super Stackers are available in four sizes: 36 by 76 inches (EBST-3676); 36 by 80 inches (EBST-3680); 39 by 76 inches (EBST-3976); and 39 by 80 inches (EBST-3980). A 12½-inch-wide, 54¾-inch-high, four-rung ladder (HB-L) with plastic-capped feet that attaches to the top bed is available. The bottom bed frame rises 12 inches from the floor, the top frame is 51 inches off the ground, there's 37 inches between the two, and the whole arrangement is 63¾ inches high and 80 or 84 inches long.

Since Super Stackers are normally sold only to institutions (like Harvard U., maybe) and not to private individuals, most dealers carrying the Harvard consumer line don't have them; but, according to a company spokesman, they can special-order them if requested to do so. The company hasn't put a suggested retail price on Super Stackers, but the same spokesman supposes that the average dealer would probably ask somewhere between $300 and $400 for them. For the name of a dealer in a particular area, write the Harvard Manufacturing Company, Bedford Heights, Ohio 45613.

Left as is, the Super Stacker leaves much to be desired in the looks department, but a bright coat of enamel—in one or many colors—could turn it into something quite special.

The Burr Folding Bed

Many, if not most, of the more unusual beds and bed-related brainchildren that found their way into the U.S. Patent Office during the past 150 years or so never found their way out to become slept-on realizations. But proof that some did end up seeing the light of day (and the dark of night) was on display at Circa Too Antiques (374 Atlantic Avenue, Brooklyn, N.Y. 11217). On sale there, exactly one hundred years after the patent for it was issued, for a mere $350, was the Burr Folding Bed, Patent 222,379, a false cabinet/desk by day, a fold-out bed by night.

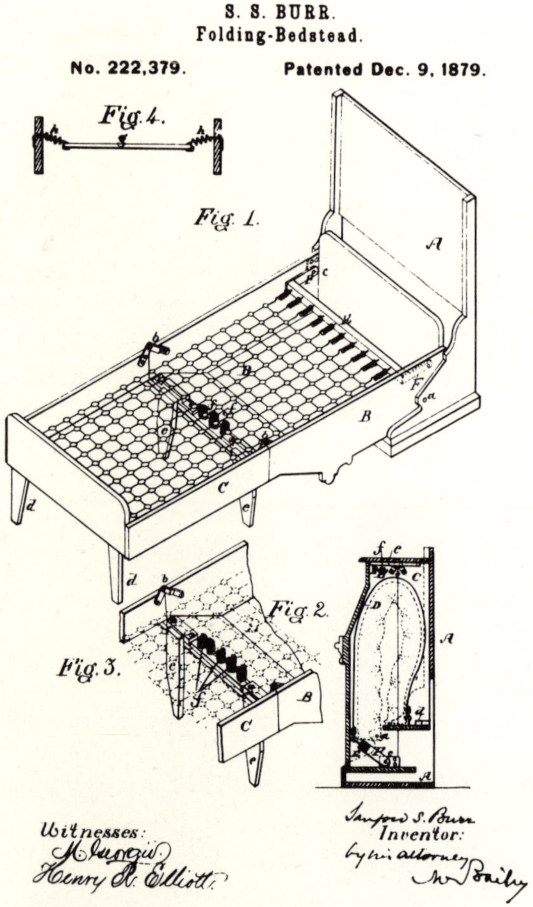

Page from Sanford S. Burr's 1879 patent for his folding bedstead.

Seal on the inside of the bed showing it to be a genuine Burr Folding Bed.

Above: *The Burr Folding Bed, folded up in front of Circa Too Antiques in Brooklyn.*

Right: *The Burr Folding Bed, folded out.*

A Reproduction Queen Anne Headboard

This is Smith & Watson's Queen Anne Headboard A-12. "In red lacquer with raised Chinese floral border. Other colors by special order." Prices (headboard alone): single (or twin), $1,510; double, $1,840; and dual (or king), $2,210. Made-to-order side and foot rails are available. See page 60.

A Reproduction Sheraton Headboard

Here is Smith & Watson's Sheraton Headboard A-20 "of bamboo detail copied from an 18th century daybed. Finished to order in wood or lacquer." Prices (for headboard alone): single (or twin), $1,310; double, $1,690; dual (or king), $2,210. Made-to-order side and foot rails are available. See page 60.

A Simulated Bamboo Tester Bed

The auction house that sold it, Sotheby Parke Bernet, estimated that Lot 325 would bring $1,000 to $2,500 when it went on the block on October 9, 1976. The catalog description was: "Regency simulated bamboo painted tester bed, first quarter 19th century. The rectangular canopy with outset rounded corners, on bamboo supports joined by a shaped headboard. Height 6 feet 5 inches (1.96 m); length 6 feet 8 inches (2.04 m); width 38½ inches (98 cm)." The estimate was a very good one, for this most interesting example of *faux bamboo* was brought in at $2,000.

The interlübke Wall System Bed

Designed in West Germany by Design Team 4, the interlübke cabinet-wall system features modular cabinet units, units with fold-down desks and tables, and a revolving cabinet unit that conceals a fold-down bed. The manufacturer says the bed unit is "an imaginative solution exclusive to interlübke, serving a double purpose when precious living space has to be gained. Ideal for guest rooms, children's rooms, flats, hotels and holiday accommodation. At night you swing the cupboard front to the rear and a comfortable bed appears, without anything having to be removed from the cupboard. A charming living room by day, a proper bedroom at night. We can also supply the interlübke cabinet-wall with double revolving beds."

The unit shown here includes shelves and a drop-down desk on the cabinet side. The reverse side contains a 36-by-75-inch bed, a night table, and a night lamp. The single slender door to the right of the revolving cabinet contains a closet which is part of the unit, the total width of which is 62 inches. The price is $2,930. The importer, International Contract Furnishings (145 East 57th Street, New York, N.Y. 10022), will sell it to you only through an architect, interior designer, or decorator.

Diagram showing the interlübke cabinet-wall revolving bed flanked by other interlübke cabinet-wall units.

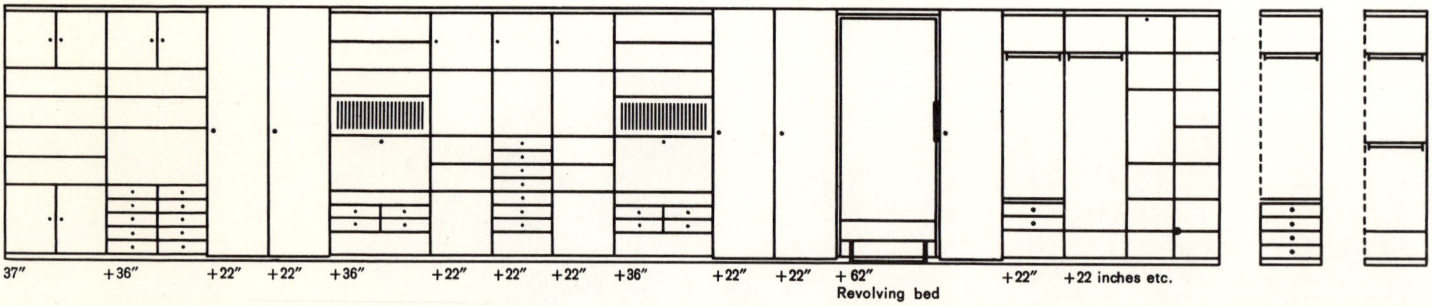

The interlübke cabinet-wall revolving bed being revolved.

The revolving bed completely revolved and folded down.

Michael Russo's "Risencrest" Bed

Michael Russo designs and makes furniture pieces that he collectively calls "Furnique." He shows his unique "Furnique" works in his Gallery Furnique (227 West 28th Street, New York, N.Y. 10001) and says the concept behind them "embodies a combination of function with visually fluid design." In "Risencrest," a typical "Furnique" design, described as "an environment of organic, rhythmic visual lines," Russo combines his fluid design concept with a most appropriate function: housing a rhythmic, fluid water-bed mattress.

And he combines an interesting assortment of materials in the construction of "Risencrest": yellow pine, Italian poplar, Plexiglas, lamp cords, eight amber-flame 7½-watt candelabra bulbs, electrical switches and connectors, ball coasters, and latex surgical tubing. Wood surfaces are finished with an oil-base enamel color tint with an alkyd, vinyl "heirloom" protective coating over that. "Risencrest" is 7 feet long, 8 feet wide, and 8 feet 3 inches high. It takes a king-size water-bed mattress.

The only thing ununique about "Risencrest" is the fact that Russo will make more than one of them—as many as he gets orders for. For $2,000 you can have a "Risencrest" of your very own.

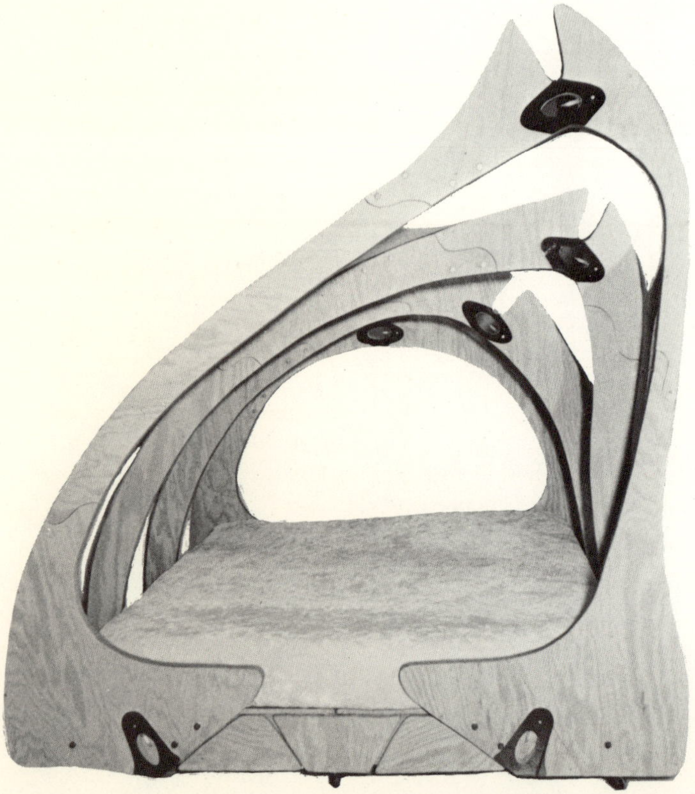

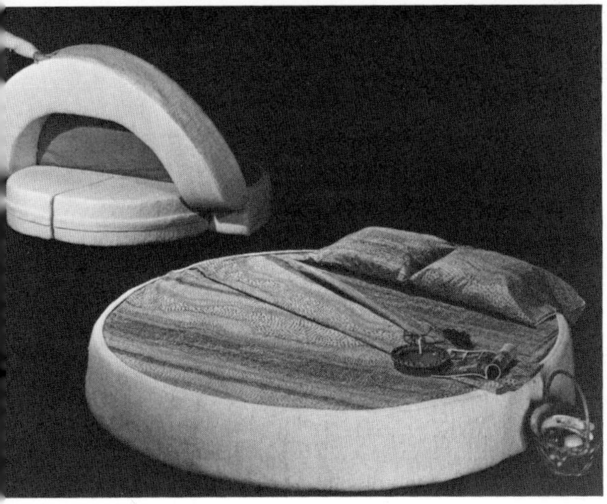

The "Round Sleeper"

"Frank W. Petersilie," says the Spherical Furniture Company brochure of SFC's founder, "broke into the furniture industry with one of the most radically different concepts in sleep-sofa, dual-purpose furniture since the early 1940s. Totally eliminating metal or wood components, he devised a convertible bed. Using the finest quality urethane mattress material, he dissected the bed into sections that allowed the bed to actually serve as a sofa by flipping one section up to serve as the back rest, and the seating void became two ottomans. Not only did he break the norms of frames and steel mechanisms, but he designed numerous shapes and sizes of convertible bedding. His first unit was the 'Round Sleeper' which shattered conventional ideas of the way sleepers had to be. This was, and still is, the only 'round' sleep-sofa in the industry."

The "Round Sleeper" has an 84-inch (measured diagonally) sleeping surface, and it is only one of a number of unusual beds in the Spherical Furniture Company line.

The "Trivertible" is a "three-in-one design that expands on the boundless possibilities of the sleep-sofa. As a curved harem-style couch, just made for two, the unit easily flips to reveal a 79-inch round bed. Replace the cushion on the open sleeping surface, and the third function becomes a giant-sized hassock."

The "Bull's Eye" is a "nine-piece seating/sleeping environment. Against the wall or floating in the center of the room, it can handle the whole family for conversation or TV, and can be modified to become a 79-inch circular bed with its own graphic [a large bull's-eye] bedspread."

The "Rendezvous" is "a circular 96-inch pit. . . . Two wedge-shaped ottomans are placed against the sofa and a table/headboard section rounds out the pit. . . . Removing the cushions and flipping the back arc to encompass the ottomans forms the world's largest round sleep-sofa."

The "Round Sleeper" will run you around $499 or more, depending on what it's covered with. You can learn the prices of the other beds described (and see what they look like) by writing to Spherical Furniture Company, Boone, N.C. 28607.

"The Nest"

A Swiss firm designed "The Nest." The U.S. importer, Turner Ltd. (305 East 63rd Street, New York, N.Y. 10021), describes it this way:

"The sofa's two leather mattresses conveniently unfold into a double bed that has a sleeping area of 174 cm (68.5 inches) by 195 cm (76.7 inches). The leather piping of the detached back cushions (supported by a chrome tubular bar) also characterizes the suite's full-foam upholstered armchairs. The sleeping sides of the mattresses are cloth-covered for comfort."

Closed, the sofa is 195 cm (76.7 inches) wide and 92 cm (36.2 inches) deep; the seat height is 40 cm (15.7 inches) and the overall height 78 cm (30.7 inches).

"The Nest" (a.k.a. DS-85) is available only through interior decorators, designers, and architects (a.k.a. "the trade"). In canvas it's $2,292; in leather it's $3,449.

A Mummy Sleeping Bag

Designer Janet Girard is seen here engaged in a mummylike tete-a-Tut in her Egyptianesque sleeping bag without peer amid pillows that match, the perfect thing for after-curfew covering up on cold nights in Cairo (or anywhere else). It's made of Dacron-filled and quilted gold lamé that's been painted by airbrush in "jewel colors": turquoise, cobalt blue, absisian black, cornelian red, and gold. Girard will make only twenty-five of the 8-foot-long bags and she's asking $2,000 for each. You can find out if any are left by writing to Girard Designs, 382 Lafayette Street, New York, N.Y. 10003.

A Cabinetmaker's Bed

Sid Fleisher of Basic Creek Woodworking made this bed, and says: "This is my version of the traditional four-poster. The clean simple lines of this piece are an influence of the early Shaker furniture builders who lived and worked in this area. I build this bed to accommodate a full- or queen-size mattress." The full-size frame is $325, the queen $350. Cherry, oak, or maple wood is used. Delivery is available to eastern New York, Massachusetts, and metropolitan New York City. The beds may also be shipped by common carrier in a reusable plywood crate for $35 plus shipping. The bed is easy to assemble; there are only four main parts: headboard, footboard, and two side rails. Additional information and a brochure may be had by writing to Sid Fleisher, Basic Creek Woodworking, Box 272, Clarksville, N.Y. 12041.

The Bureau Bed

If you think this is a nice bed with four drawers underneath, you're wrong. It has eight—four on one side and four more on the other. A Low Bureau Bed is also available; it has four drawers, two on each side. A twin-size Bureau Bed can be had two ways: high with four drawers on one side or low with two drawers on one side. They're all types of captain's beds, but the eight-drawer model might be better described as an admiral's.

Two other interesting things about the Bureau Bed: it collapses, and it comes in a box with humorous assembly instructions.

The eight-drawer bed is $630 in birch or oak and $695 in walnut for a three-quarter-size mattress, $645 and $725 for a full, $670 and $745 for a queen, and $740 and $815 for a king. The manufacturer will send prices for the other sizes on request—and, if you ask real nice, they might even throw in a set of their funny instructions. Write Loftcraft, 171 Seventh Avenue, New York, N.Y. 10011.

A Reproduction Pencil-Post Bed

From the Bury Farm catalog:

"We have been in the antiques business for many years, operating a cabinet shop along with our antiques shop. This has given us excellent experience in the restoration and refinishing of many fine antiques. Requests from customers made us aware of the need for a period bed that would not look like the usual commercial reproduction and would provide modern comfort in the contemporary sizes. Advertising nationally has proven this need exists and our beds have gone into some of the earliest homes of New England and as far as Texas and Oregon.

"The bed design we use faithfully copies a lovely 18th-century museum example having a simple headboard. The slender octagonal posts feature a lamb's tongue detail where posts square off to the bottom. Posts are made up to a graceful 7½-foot height and taper to a slender 1 inch at top. Each bed is custom made and post height can be adjusted as needed. Even shorter posts are graceful since they are planed to a 1-inch top. Posts are solid wood—not laminated.

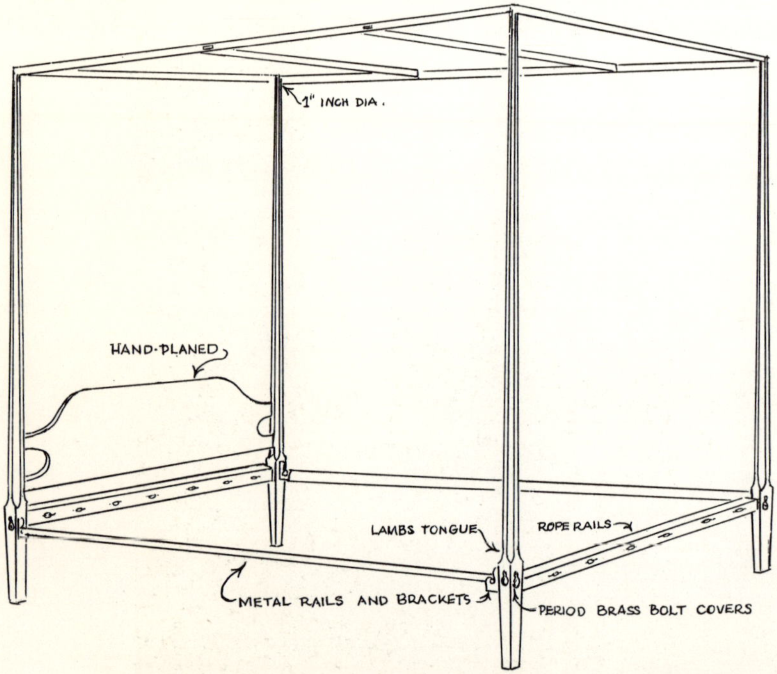

Diagram showing the different parts of Richard Bury's 18th-century pencil-post bed reproduction.

"Handmade rope rails at the head and foot add an authentic touch. They can be laced with rope. Metal side-rails are supplied unless wooden rope rails are preferred. The top of standard bedding averages 30 inches from the floor when the bed is made up, giving the appearance of an old bed.

"Each bed is made entirely by hand of native maple or cherry and finished in hand-rubbed natural wood tones. Antique red or blue painted finish is also available at the same price."

A twin, three-quarter, or double bed is $350; a queen-size is $375; a king is $475. Limited orders for tiger maple are accepted. The starting price in that wood is $850. All king-size beds are made with wooden side rails and center support. Delivery takes eight months to a year.

A brochure describing this reproduction bed in greater detail is available for the asking. Write to Bury Farm Antiques, Morrisville, N.Y. 13408.

The "Generation Hammock"

A lot of people around the world, notably the inhabitants of some of the more remote regions of South America's interior, sleep exclusively in hammocks. However attractive the idea of bedding down nightly in a hammock might be, however, most of us would find it far less comfortable than the solid horizontal surface we grew up with. The "Generation Hammock" made by Tom and Anne Hoopes of Rust Pond Workshop might be just the compromise a lot of frustrated hammock-sleepers have been waiting for.

"This hammock," writes Tom Hoopes in the Rust Pond catalog, "is a copy of a turn-of-the-century hammock. I have repaired and replaced so many of these old torn and dilapidated hammocks that I finally started to make them. . . . Made with the quality workmanship that existed at the turn of the century, this hammock is a rugged and functional addition to family comfort. It is not so much a hammock as it is a hanging bed. The heavy 22-ounce canvas is suspended from heavy steel rings by ropes at each end, given shape by a roped oak frame, and cushioned by a 4-inch foam pad. The cushion cover has a long zipper to facilitate removal for washing. The hammock is intended for sheltered use, on a porch or as indoor furniture, as the heavy canvas does not come with a mildew-resistant finish."

The hammock body is available in natural canvas only. The cushions are available in tan, navy, or brown. The "Generation Hammock" is 6 feet long, 6 inches thick, and 30 inches wide, and weighs 50 pounds. It sells for $225. Shipment (by truck) adds about $20. To order, or for more information and a free Rust Pond Workshop catalog, write to Rust Pond Workshop, RFD #1, Box 53A, East Alton, N.H. 03809.

A Low-Profile "Knock-down" Pine Bed

A bed that arrives "KD," which is furniture industry jargon for "knocked down," is this all-pine, low-profile example from the Sugar Hill Furniture division of the Plymwood Furniture Corporation, Lisbon, N.H. 03585. Designated no. 1410 in Sugar Hill's "Dartmouth Collection," it sells for around $291 in queen-size, a price that's more likely to be knocked up than down in some parts of the country. The available finishes are a dark brown antique, a lighter honey tone, and a grayish "Tavern." A list of names of dealers in your region who can sell you a box with a knocked-down 1410 inside is available from the manufacturer.

Canopy Bed Plans to Send For

You can make this canopy bed from full-sized plans available from Furniture Designs in Illinois. Furniture Designs says: "Here is a plan for a project worthy of any woodworker's talents. This Canopy Bed has been designed after careful research to embody all the features desired in such a piece. Even the blanket rail found on many Colonial beds has been included. The posts are designed to be turned in sections in order that they may fit in the average home lathe. It may be made as either a twin or full-size bed. The plan also includes full-size details of the arched canopy or tester frame. Omit the canopy if you prefer and you have a beautiful 71½-inch-high poster bed. Height overall with the canopy frame is 80½ inches."

About all their woodworking plans, Furniture Designs says: "Since the plans are *full-size*, you are able to save time! There is no need to enlarge plans from small scale to full-size. No cutting and pasting-up of pattern is required. You can trace your patterns onto your work directly from the *full-size* plan. All guesswork is eliminated. A complete list of materials, including hardware, is on each plan, saving time in gathering the necessary parts. We suggest and show proper joints. In addition, an 'exploded' perspective sketch will show at a glance how all parts are assembled."

The Canopy Bed plan is no. 145. It will be sent to you if you send $8 to Furniture Designs, 1425 Sherman Avenue, Evanston, Ill. 60201. For $1 they'll send a catalog of 150 different plans. See also pages 48 and 71.

A Reproduction Sheraton Four-Poster

Right: *Sheraton poster bed reproduction from Reid Classics. It's their no. 6600—a combination of their post 6000, headboard 600, and tester frame 22C. The Reid Classics catalog asks that you "note the fine arched and molded tester."*

Below: *A close look at the bed bolt construction feature used to assemble Reid Classics reproduction beds.*

From the Reid Classics catalog:

"The introduction of genuine mahogany to European craftsmen created an inspiration that brought on a new era of furniture design, abruptly ending the heavy, grotesque style that prevailed when only native woods were used. It is for this reason that we choose genuine Honduras mahogany as our standard material [for constructing beds] . . . since almost all of them were built with the same majestic wood by the masters who first created them.

"At the same time, some of the designs herein lend themselves equally well to the characteristics of other woods and for this reason we can usually furnish any bed in cherry, maple, walnut, or birch, at slightly additional cost. . . .

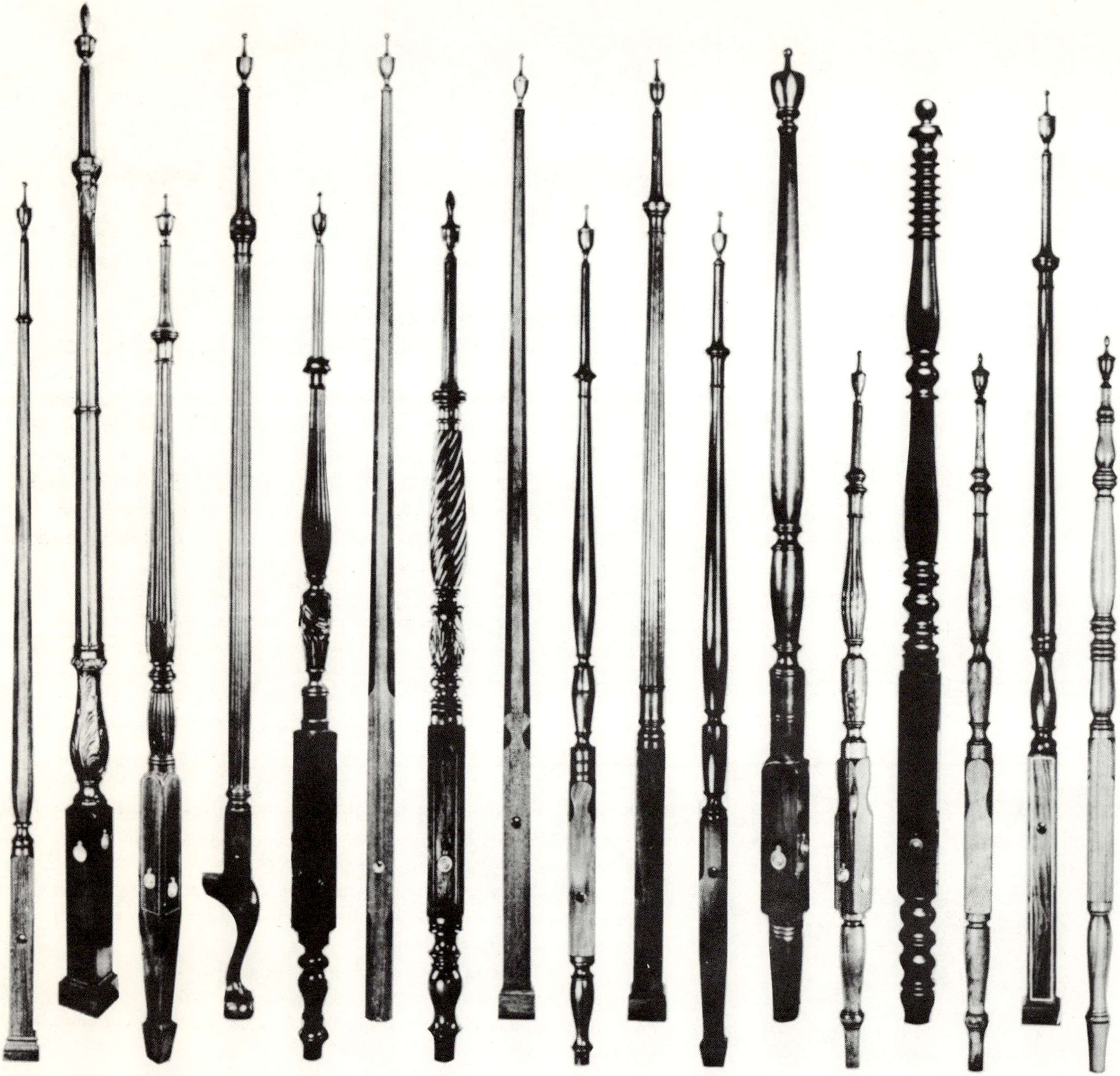

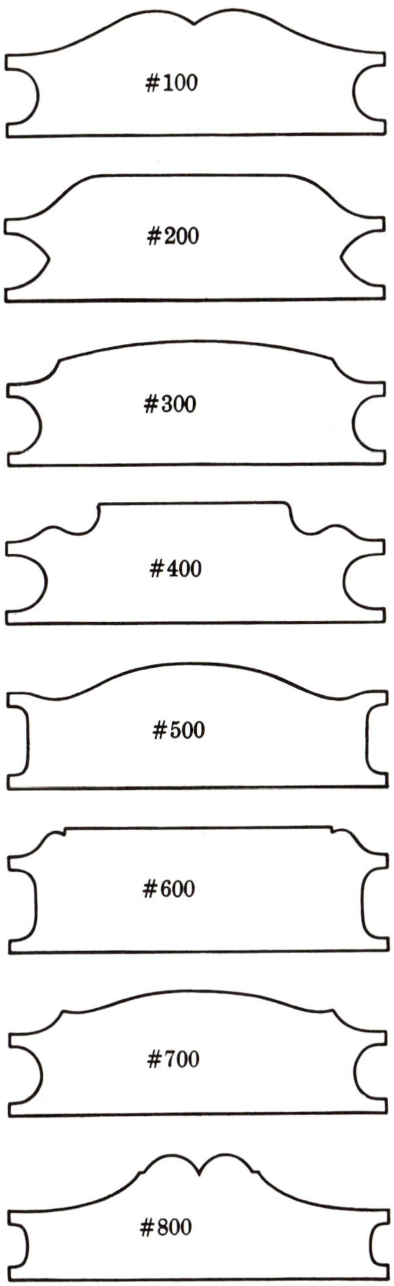

"Each Reid Classic mahogany bed is the true color of the authentic antique from which it was reproduced, which means that the color of the hand-rubbed soft finish may vary from the dark, rich brown of Victorian models to lighter fruitwood tones of Colonial pieces. We will furnish other tones on special request. . . .

"As you assemble any of these beds you will be impressed with the heft of the rails and the manner of locking rail to post. The rails on all tall posters are dressed out of stock of thickness 2 inches or more. The rails on the short posters average 1¾ inches by 4 inches. . . .

"The bed bolt construction feature is most important: having spent years in the repair and finishing of fine furniture (as well as building it) we are familiar with the many methods of assembling beds. The bolt construction we use on all beds is the only method that simply never fails—and we have seen it on beds as old as 200 years! The 2-inch-thick side rails are solid mahogany and a heavy nut is imbedded to receive the bolt, tightening the rails into place. Cast brass covers conceal the holes. . . .

"All beds are made to fit either standard single or double size modern springs and mattresses."

Reid Classics' no. 6600 is 83 inches high and costs $2,037. If you don't care for the 6600's headboard, you can substitute another for it, and the same goes for the posts. There are seventeen different Reid Classics posts and eight headboards to choose from. They will take any post and combine four of them (or two of one kind and two of another) with any headboard for a "made-to-order" reproduction of your choice. Three to six weeks is the time Reid Classics normally requires to make a bed and ship it.

The Reid Classics catalog contains scores of reproduction beds; it can be obtained by sending $2 to Reid Classics, 3600 Old Shell Road, P.O. Box 8383, Mobile, Ala. 36608.

See also pages 127 and 149.

Seventeen Reid Classics post styles combine with eight different headboards for 136 different possible combinations—and that's assuming all four of each bed's posts are the same!

The Navona Sleep Sofa

Of their no. 050 Navona Seating Series the people at The Pace Collection Inc. (321 East 62nd Street, New York, N.Y. 10021) say: "The lounge chair, sofas, corner unit, one-arm units, and armless modular units are available with or without bed units, both resulting in a visually exciting, extremely comfortable seating series. Upholstery is available in leather, suede, and a wide variety of imported fabrics."

The 050 Lounge Chair, in what Pace calls its "P" fabric, is $2,190 and closed measures 41 inches wide by 34¾ inches deep by 29 inches high. The 050/3 Three Seat Sofa in the same fabric is $4,135 and closed measures 95¾ inches wide by 34¾ inches deep by 29 inches high.

Pace sells only to "the trade" (interior designers, decorators, and architects) and, in addition to the one in New York, has showrooms in Chicago, Los Angeles, Miami, Boston, Dallas, San Francisco, and Seattle.

A three-seat sofa and matching lounge chair that turn into . . .

. . . a large bed and a matching small bed. They're part of The Pace Collection's no. 050 Navona Seating Series.

The "803" Chaise Lounge

Most chaise longues are much more chair than bed, but the no. 803 Chaise Lounge from The Pace Collection Inc. (321 East 62nd Street, New York, N.Y. 10021) seems to be a rare exception, more suitable for lying down or sleeping than for sitting.

"The 803 Chaise Lounge," says Pace, "is the last word in contemporary relaxation. Quintessential in design, the 803 Chaise is distinguished by a polished chrome frame topped with a luxurious foam cushion and matching pillow. Available in Pace's own imported suedes, leathers, or fabrics."

It's 33 inches wide and 75 inches long, has a seat height of 16½ inches, and can be had (but only through the interior decorators, designers, and architects who make up "the trade") in leather or suede for $2,145. In addition to the one in New York, Pace Collection showrooms are located in Chicago, Los Angeles, Miami, Boston, Dallas, San Francisco, and Seattle.

A Reproduction Sheraton Turned Bed

From the Douglas Campbell Company catalog:

"We are a small company with the most extraordinary capability of copying the whole variety of fine American antiques from the 17th and 18th centuries. This unique service is possible due to our emphasis on knowledge of the furniture, the mechanics of our craft, and many years of the most comprehensive experience. As we reflect on our past, we have been extremely competitive by not specializing in several items as most small shops have and not 'engineering' furniture for the convenience of manufacturing and packaging as have the larger companies. We have not and never will manufacture standard items to be peddled by merchants.

"Although our furniture exceeds the quality and accuracy of occasional competitors for your attention, we take great pride in our attitudes regarding reproductions. The great American furniture designs, and the techniques required to make them, are not lost or difficult to comprehend by the interested, well-trained craftsman. Our diligence, knowledge, and sensitivity to detail have given us the success that will sustain this great opportunity to serve the public for many generations to come.

"The illustrations and dimensions . . . are examples only. Each piece is made from the wood and to the size requested. If we feel that the choice could be improved, we will offer our opinion. Please feel free to use any book as a reference. All drawings and pictures will be returned. Items not catalogued will be quoted on, promptly. All quotes will include packing and shipping costs.

"All beds are shipped unassembled along with bed bolts, wrench, and brackets to support a box spring."

The bed shown here is 81 inches high at the top of the arch. The height at the top of the rails is 20 inches. It is made from maple and stained to order. A single or double bed is $755. A queen is $775.

The Douglas Campbell Co. has two addresses: Denmark, Me. 04022, and 31 Bridge Street, Newport, R.I. 02840. A request sent to either address, along with $2, will get you a copy of the complete Douglas Campbell furniture catalog.

See also pages 66 and 115.

A "hired man's bed" reproduced by the Douglas Campbell Company. It is 36 inches high at its highest point and 18½ inches at the top of the rails. The wood is maple, painted with red milk paint or stained to order. A single bed is $390; a queen is $410. A king-size hired man's bed, which is an interesting and decidedly contradictory combination, is $430. See page 114.

A Reproduction "Hired Man's Bed"

The High-Tech Bed

Redroof Design (9-01 44th Drive, Long Island City, N.Y. 11101) designer Yann Weymouth took some slotted angles (heavy L-shaped metal units that bolt together to create heavy-duty industrial shelving, partitions, and scaffolding) and fashioned from them a canopy bed that was very much in keeping with the style that's come to be called High Tech (an approach to interior design that incorporates materials and objects more at home at construction sites and factories than in the home). A best-selling book of the same name featured Weymouth's bed, and Macy's, "the world's largest department store" on Herald Square in New York (N.Y. 10001), in keeping with their Seventh Avenue dress manufacturing neighbors' tradition of "knocking off" inexpensive versions of Paris originals, knocked it off. Contracting a steel locker maker to do the manufacturing, they've come out with a slotted angle canopy bed that's the twin of Weymouth's. Selling for $225, it's 87 inches long, almost as high (86 inches), and 67 inches wide. Does Yann Weymouth mind? Not at all; in fact, he says, he's honored.

A Contemporary Brass and Cast-Iron Bed

Two craftsmen showed their true metal when brass-bed maker Joao Isabel and iron forger/metalsmith Tom Markusen linked up to design this one-of-a-kind brass and forged-iron bed. A star attraction in 1978 at the Sixth International Craft Show held at the New York Coliseum, the bed is now in the possession of Markusen, who lives and works near Rochester, N.Y. And it's for sale. The price: $10,000. For more information contact Joao Isabel, 120 East 32nd Street, New York, N.Y. 10016. (See page 52.)

A Billionaire's 17th-Century English Bed

What would it be like to sleep every night on a bed that was slept on by one of the richest men who ever lived? You could have found out had you outbid the person who paid $9,900—at an auction held on May 31, 1978, at Christie, Manson & Woods International Inc. (a.k.a. Christie's), 502 Park Avenue, New York, N.Y. 10022—for the bed shown here. It belonged to the late billionaire J. Paul Getty. The auction catalog described it as a "James I [1603–1625] Oak and Marquetry four-post canopy bed. Property offered by the Executors of the Estate of J. Paul Getty. Early 17th century. 57½ inches (146 cm) by 91 inches (231 cm)."

This sleigh bed was sold at an important three-day auction (held on November 16, 17, and 18, 1978), by Sotheby Parke Bernet. The catalog estimated that the bed might fetch between $7,000 and $9,000 and carried the following write-up: "Extremely rare and important classical brass-mounted mahogany, giltwood, and gesso bed, Labeled and Branded by Charles Honoré Lannuier, New York, circa 1815, having S-scrolled head- and footboards, the headboard with gilt eagle capitals, the terminals with *repoussé* pressed brass plaques, the plain frame on gilded paw feet with leaf-carved capitals. Height 42½ inches (1.08 m); length 8 feet (2.44 m); width 57¼ inches (1.45 m). . . . This sleigh bed belonged to Alfred Seton, partner of John Jacob Astor and nephew of the Saint, Mother Elizabeth Seton."

Someone found all that information impressive enough to make a final and winning bid of $19,000 for the bed.

An 1815 American Sleigh Bed

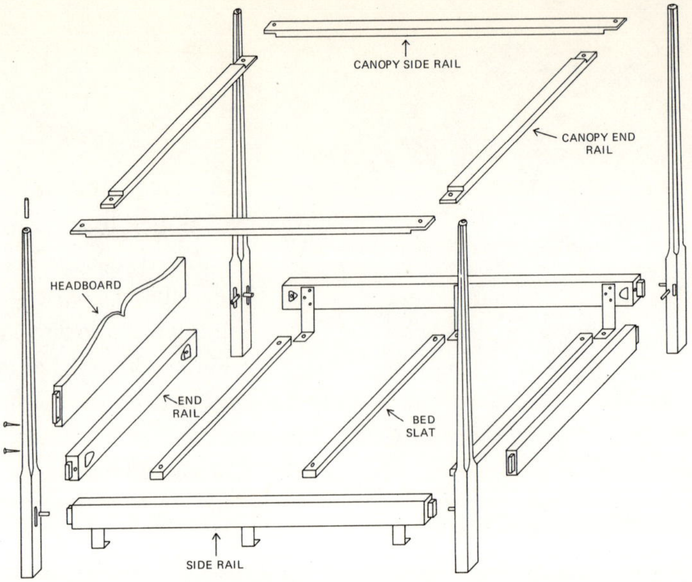

"Exploded" diagram showing the Bartley Collection pencil-post bed kit's individual parts.

Like bock beer and tickets to the Super Bowl, the Bartley Collection pencil-post bed (c. 1750 New England) kit is available only for a short period each year. Each fall, "one cutting only" is made of this bed. "Brought from Exeter, New Hampshire, the original is in the Secretary House in Greenfield Village [Dearborn, Michigan]," explains the Bartley Collection catalog. "It is prized there because of its perfect proportions and rarity. The original is approximately double-bed size. We have carefully scaled the headboard so that we offer it in three sizes. Equally striking with or without the canopy. In either Pennsylvania Cherry or Honduras Mahogany."

The bed comes two ways: in its unassembled, ready-to-finish kit form, and already assembled and finished. As a single bed (approximately 82 inches long by 44 inches wide by 83 inches high), the kit is $325; assembled and finished it's $825. The double bed (approximately 82 inches long by 60 inches wide by 83 inches high) kit is $385; the assembled and finished bed is $900. Queen-size (approximately 87 inches long by 66 inches wide by 83 inches high) bed kits go for $430, $1,025 being the price of the assembled and finished bed of that size. Each bed is made to order, so 90 to 120 days should be allowed on kits, six to twelve months on a finished bed. Kits and assembled beds are shipped "freight collect."

To order a bed or request a free Bartley Collection catalog, write to The Bartley Collection, Ltd., 121 Schelter Road, Prairie View, Ill. 60069.

A Pencil-Post Bed Kit

A Sleeping Bag Kit

You can put more of yourself into this sleeping bag than into most others, because you make it yourself. It's a kit from Country Ways, a small company in Minnesota that makes kits for everything from jackets and backpacks to snowshoes, musical instruments, and, of course, sleeping bags.

Country Ways says about all their kits: "We've done the really tough stuff, but we've left the true 'making' for you. You get to cut the pieces—more accurately than a machine—and you get to alter, adapt and customize at will." And about their sleeping bag kits specifically: "Our directions suggest a 'modified taper' shape—just roomy enough to roll over without taking the bag with you. Each kit can, however, be made to any shape, from extreme mummy to rectangular. Our bags zip together (even different sizes), and also open flat to serve as a quilt. . . . Each bag has a full hood and drawstring, and the shoulder area tapers toward the hood to prevent bunching when the hood is closed. Zippers are full length, two-way and reversible."

Country Ways also explains that their sleeping bag kits come in different warmths. Summer—"comfortable for many from the 70s into the 40s." Three Seasons—"from 60 into the 20s. This is our most popular bag because of its flexibility and warmth under most all camping conditions." Extra Warm—"from the 40s to about 0°, for fall, winter and spring use." A sufficient amount of Polar Guard insulation for the warmth desired is included in each kit.

In addition to three different warmths, Country Ways sleeping bag kits come in three different sizes: medium—for people 4 feet 6 inches to 5 feet 7 inches tall; standard—to 6 feet 2 inches; long—to 6 feet 8 inches. Kit prices vary according to warmth and size. A medium-size Summer bag is $45; a standard is $48; a long is $51. The Three Seasons is $49, $52, and $55. The Extra Warm is $53, $56, and $60.

A request and a dollar sent to Country Ways, 3500 Highway 101 South, Minnetonka, Minn. 55343, will bring the sender the complete Country Ways kit catalog.

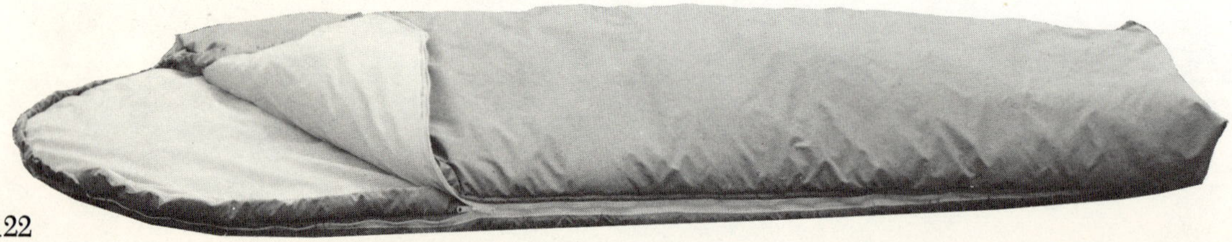

A Bed with a Leather and Feather Bedspread

Sometimes the most interesting thing about an interesting bed is its bedspread. The otherwise unremarkable bed shown here, because it is under a very remarkable leather and feather spread designed and executed by artist Jeremie Hawley, is a case and matching pillowcase in point.

The bedspread's feathers—hackle and wild turkey—are removable. The leather is elk. Hawley, himself half American Indian, half of that half being Cherokee and the other half Pawnee, used acrylic colors to render a half-portrait of a Hopi Indian woman in the center of the spread, an image he repeated in the assemblage hanging above the bed.

This spread, which measures 74 by 108 inches (standard twin or single), is an original that sold for $1,200. Requests for information regarding other one-of-a-kind Jeremie Hawley bedspreads should be addressed to Made On Earth, 1745 Correa Way, Brentwood, Calif. 94513.

"Series Ring" Beds from Campus

Putting together a "Series Ring" single bed.

Some devilish minds working for a company called Campus in Brescia, Italy, have come up with an ingenious modular system from which a number of beautiful beds can be constructed. Called "Series Ring," it consists of a number of gaily painted metal tubes that connect by means of die-cast aluminum fittings—straight ones for joining two tubes end-to-end and branching ones for joining three tubes meeting at a corner. Beds with high headboards and high footboards, or high headboards and low footboards, or low headboards and low footboards can be put together, depending on the parts packed inside the surprisingly small box each bed comes in. More tubes can be joined to add on to any bed an almost infinite variety of useful wall units. And a canvas canopy can be added to a bed with a high head and foot to create a very exciting "four-poster" canopy bed.

Ambienti (792 Madison Avenue, New York, N.Y. 10021) is the exclusive United States importer of "Series Ring." Prices range from around $300 to around $600, depending on the size of the bed and the number of components required to put it together. Single beds are presently available in red, yellow, and blue with fittings in the same colors. Queen- and king-size beds are presently available in the United States only in black with chrome joints. Sufficient consumer interest in "Series Ring," says Ambienti, will result in increased color options and a larger selection of add-on units.

"Series Ring" single bed put together.

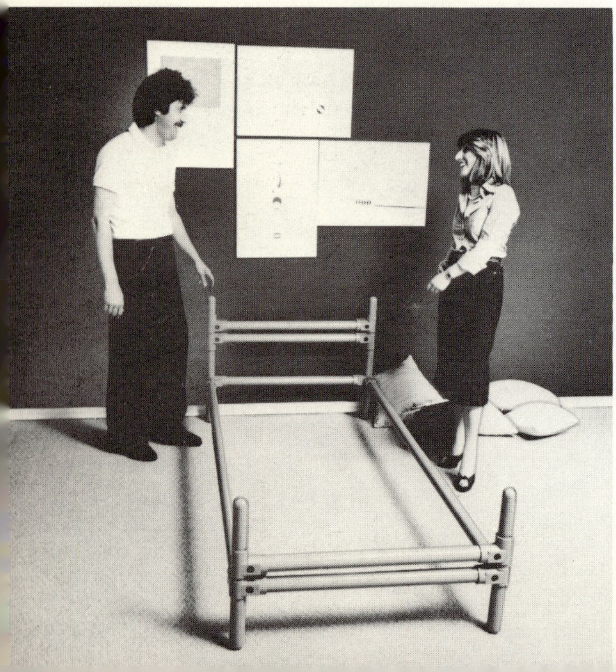

"Series Ring" four-poster with canopy.

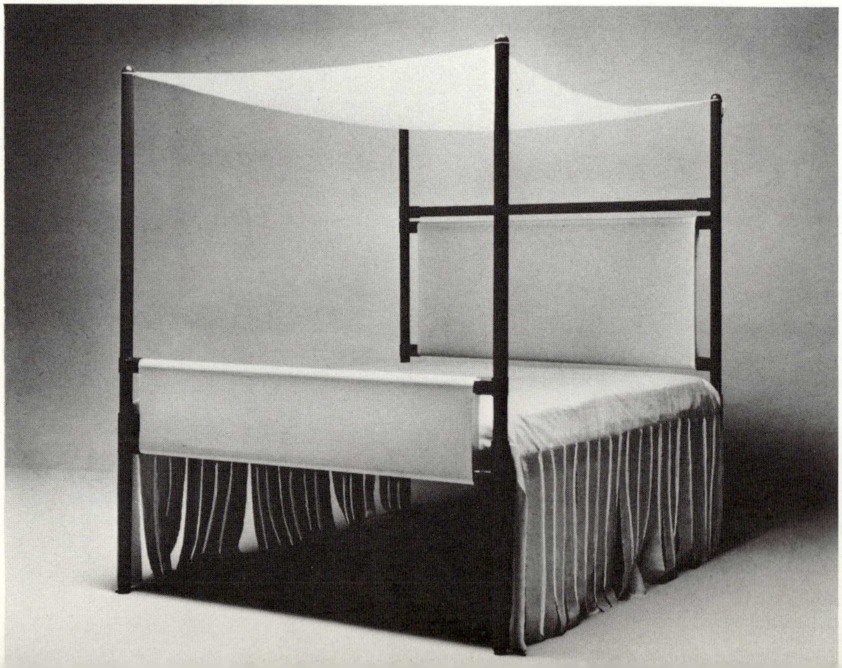

"Series Ring" bed with add-on components attached.

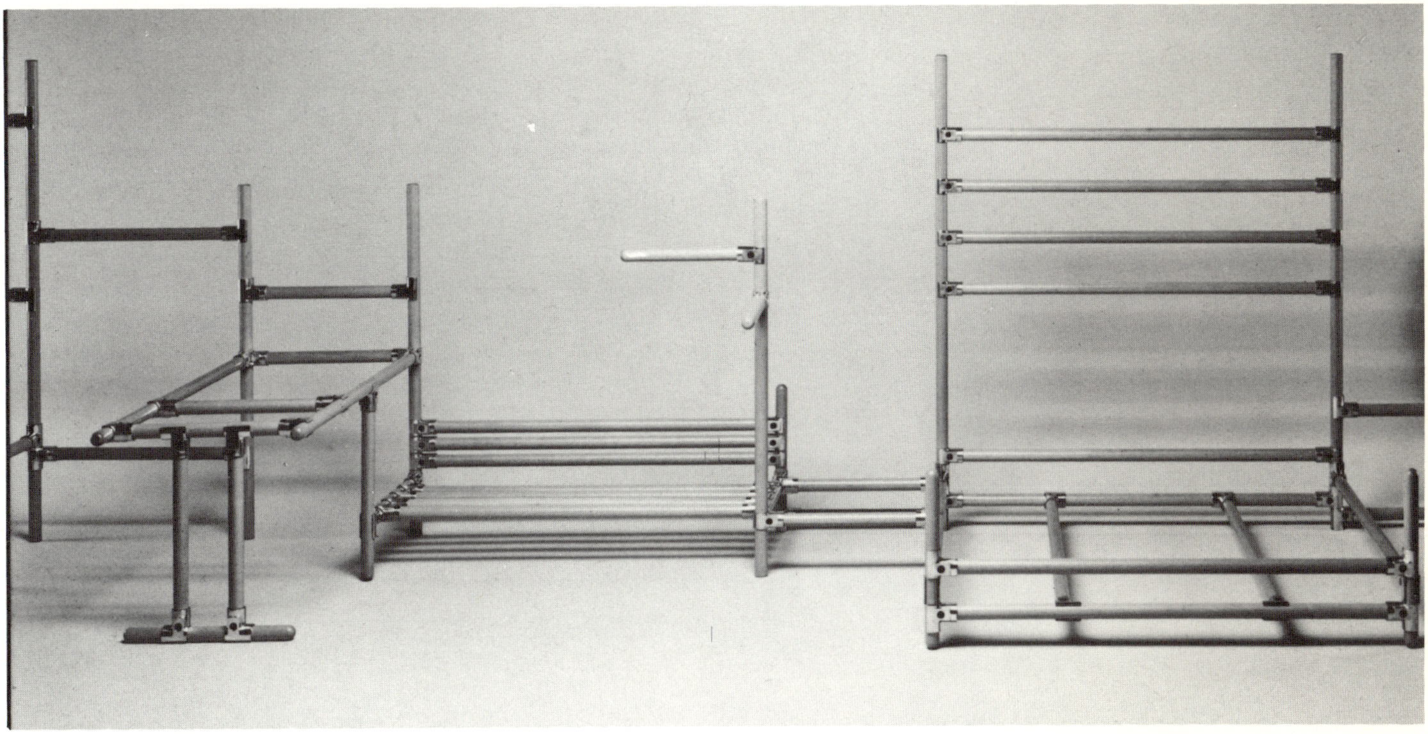

"Series Ring" queen-size bed with low head and low foot.

"Series Ring" queen-size bed with low foot, high head, and two children.

"An important mahogany & burl walnut double bed by Louis Majorelle, c. 1895; part of a 7-piece bedroom suite, including armoire, dressing table, all *en suite* and inlaid with fruit woods, purple heart and mother-of-pearl." Sold at an auction of Art Nouveau and Art Deco held at Christie's (Christie, Manson & Woods International Inc., 502 Park Avenue, New York, N.Y. 10022) on September 22 and 23, 1978, this bed, along with its *en suite* companions, went for a mere $14,300.

An Art Nouveau Bed

An "Old English" Bed Reproduction

Here is Reid Classics' Old English Bed no. CD300 (combining their posts C and D, headboard no. 300, and tester frame no. 505). It is 85 inches high and sells for $1,823. See page 109.

A Murphy Bed

Over the years, a lot of different folding beds have been mistakenly called Murphy beds, including some that came along a long time before Lawrence Murphy took out his first patents on his innovative bed system around the turn of the century. But the truth is the Murphy Door Bed Company, which is still making Murphy beds and being run by third- and fourth-generation Murphys, never made a bed that folded up. The Murphy bed is, and always has been, a rigid frame that tilts up from a horizontal position to a vertical one and hides away behind a door or in a cabinet. A counterbalancing spring system—Lawrence Murphy's major innovation and the heart of every Murphy bed—makes it possible to raise or lower the bed frame with minimum effort.

Some of the early Murphy "In-A-Dor" beds left the room completely when not in use; they had their own closets. When the closet door was opened, the vertical bed, held upright by a hinge attached to the door jamb, swung out of the closet and into the room and then down to the floor. (See pages 26–27.) Today's Murphy bed, however, is most often put out of the way behind the doors of some sort of upright cabinet.

Lew Raynes, Inc., an independent company that shares office and showroom space with the Murphy Door Bed Company at 40 East 34th Street, New York, N.Y. 10016, makes cabinets that Murphy beds disappear into. The top-of-the-line Lew Raynes cabinet (shown) is ebony-finished with hand-etched solid brass hardware and goes for $660 when a

Ebony-finished birch cabinet and matching end units from Lew Raynes, Inc., with an upended queen-size Murphy bed concealed inside.

double-size Murphy frame goes in it, and $715 when it's big enough to accommodate a queen. Matching end units (shown) are $627 each. Less expensive cabinets finished in a high-pressure laminate, such as Formica, are $530 for a double and $555 for a queen; matching side units are $503.

Into Lew Raynes cabinets go genuine Murphy bed frames. A double-size frame that attaches, as do all Murphy frames, directly to the floor and not to the cabinet—thereby eliminating the possibility of lowering the cabinet along with the bed—and equipped with a special 4-inch foundation pad runs $253.35. In a queen size (shown) it's $295.65. Without the special pad—which means you provide a board or something else to put a mattress on—the double-size frame costs $139.65. The same thing in queen is $156.95.

So, put a queen-size Murphy frame with foundation pad ($295.65) into a top-of-the-line Lew Raynes queen-size cabinet ($715) with a matching end unit ($627) on each side, and the price would come to $2,264.65. Add to that the cost of a mattress, and you're all set.

Lew Raynes ships cabinets and end units all over the country, and the Murphy Door Bed Company does the same with their frames. But there are lots of regional Murphy frame distributors around the country and quite a few companies making cabinets. The Murphy people will be glad to send the names and addresses of distributors and cabinet suppliers to anyone who writes and asks for them.

The Murphy bed revealed.

Rustic Beds by Ken Heitz

The American Log Bunk Beds can be made of maple or ash (peeled or unpeeled). Price: $1,600.

The Couch Bed, Single or Studio, is made of ash, maple, or ironwood (peeled or unpeeled). Price: $1,200.

Heitz's King-Size Canopy Bed is made of maple or ash (peeled or unpeeled). Price: $2,000.

Opposite: *Two beds constructed in the rustic style by Ken Heitz, standing outside the general store in Indian Lake, N.Y. Heitz beds are constructed with hand-carved joinery and ironwood pegs.*

Ken Heitz lives and works in the wildest part of the United States east of the Rockies, the Adirondacks, making "rustic" (also called "twig" and "Adirondacks") furniture—mostly chairs, tables, and beds—using techniques that date from around the early 1860s, when often affluent summer vacationers first began adventuring into this still-rugged region of New York State. Heitz uses no power tools. With only an ax, handsaw, jackknife, hand auger, drawknife, and rasp, he turns white ash, maple, tag alder, ironwood, balsam, and spruce into furniture with an appearance that depends as much on the natural shape of the wood as on the imagination of its maker. All of Ken Heitz's joinery is hand-carved, and all pegs are handmade ironwood.

Rustic furniture is made in one of two ways: with wood that's been peeled of its bark, or with wood with its bark left on. The bark type is for individuals who want their rustic furniture really rustic. The peeled variety is clearly more suited to most contemporary interiors.

Shown are five beds Ken Heitz would like to make for anyone interested. The drawings are by Heitz's wife, Linda.

Parrish Woodworth, Inc., 33 East 65th Street, New York, N.Y. 10021, is the sole seller of Ken Heitz beds, and they will be glad to handle orders for any of the beds shown, for interior decorators, designers, and architects only.

The Forest Double Bed can be made of maple, ash, or ironwood. Price: $1,500.

The A-Frame Log Bed, Double, is made of maple or ash (peeled or unpeeled). Price: $900.

A Pine "Farmhouse Bed"

This homey pine bed is called the Farmhouse Bed (or model no. 1801) by the people who make it—Sugar Hill Furniture, part of the Plymwood Furniture Corporation, Lisbon, N.H. 03585. Dark brown antique, a lighter honey tone, and a grayish "Tavern" are the three available finishes, and it takes a queen-size (5/0) metal frame. The price, which is slightly higher in some parts of the country, is around $1,076. Who sells it where can be found out by requesting that information from the manufacturer.

An All-Pine Bed with a High Blanket Rail

This all-pine Colonial-style four-poster bed has a handsome high blanket rail. Although this queen-size model (no. 1806) has no tester, Sugar Hill Furniture (a division of the Plymwood Furniture Corporation, Lisbon, N.H. 03585) calls it a tester bed. The price is $430 or slightly higher, depending on where it's sold. Three finishes are available: dark brown antique, honey, and the grayish "Tavern." For a list of dealers in your area selling this unique topless tester bed, drop a line to the manufacturer.

Max Ernst's "Cage Bed"

The late great German painter, sculptor, and collagist Max Ernst is perhaps best remembered as one of the artists who, in the middle of the 1920s, founded Surrealism, an art movement that drew much of its inspiration from the world of dreams. Almost exactly a half century after Surrealism began, Max Ernst finally got around to designing the perfect environment for dreaming surrealist dreams—his "Cage Bed." It was a limited edition "published" in 1975; twenty-nine beds were made.

The overall length of the bed is 8 feet 10 inches. The headboard and footboard are 7 feet 6 inches high and 8 feet 4 inches wide. The 13-inch-thick mattress is 72 inches wide by 88 inches long. African walnut is used in the footboard and headboard, and the tree branch growing out of the footboard is alder painted green. The metal rods in the foot and head are varnished ⅝-inch-diameter brass. Mirrors at the head of the bed and at the foot swivel 360 degrees and are decorated on the back by lithographs signed by Max Ernst. A lateral trap door at each side of the bed opens to reveal a telephone and a bedside lamp. The 90-inch-by-74-inch bed cover is made of mink and decorated with a drawing by the artist. The screen next to the bed is 6 feet 2⅜ inches high and 5 feet 6⅜ inches wide; an eighteen-color lithograph by the artist covers the bottom half of the central panel.

The late Nelson Rockefeller bought a "Cage Bed"; he moved it into the vice-presidential residence in Washington, D.C., took it with him when he left, and then eventually sold it. That one and twenty-eight more are out there somewhere. Perhaps someone wants to sell one. The asking price may be a lot more than the original $35,000. But who knows?

A Reproduction Palm-Post Headboard

Smith & Watson's Palm Post Headboard A-65 was "inspired by the Brighton Pavilion. Hand-carved and finished to order in wood or lacquer. Available with upholstered panel." Prices (headboard alone): single (or twin), $3,010; double, $3,400; dual (or king), $3,840. Made-to-order side and foot rails are available. See page 60.

A Broken Pediment Bed

The Sugar Loaf Broken Pediment Bed from Sugar Hill Furniture (Plymwood Furniture Corp., Lisbon, N.H. 03585) is made of pure pine. It can be had in a dark brown antique finish, a lighter honey color, or the grayer "Tavern." Any way you like it, it's around $430 (slightly higher in some parts of the country). It will take either a full (4/6) or queen-size (5/0) metal frame. The maker will tell you who sells it—it's their model 405—where, if you drop them a line.

A Federal Tester Bed

Sotheby Parke Bernet auctioned off this bed on September 30, 1978. It was Lot 364, and the catalog described it this way: "Fine Federal turned curly maple and maple tester bedstead, New England, probably Rhode Island, 1780–90, having slender ring-turned and tapered headposts centering a scroll-carved headboard, the footposts conformingly turned, on four square tapering legs ending in spade feet. Headboard restored. Has tester hangings. Height 6 feet 7 inches (2.01 m); length 6 feet 5½ inches (1.97 m); width 54 inches (1.37 m)."

The presale estimate of what the bed might bring was $4,000 to $5,000. It went for $3,750.

Antique Beds from an Antique Bed Dealer

This assortment of photographs is representative of those Valentim Mendes will send to any serious antique-bed seeker. Mr. Mendes has been selling antique beds, restored and refinished to take standard-size modern bedding, or in their original sizes with the old paint and finish, for over twenty years. The beds usually date from 1790 to 1830, and he always has a hundred or more in stock at any given time. Lowpost beds and four-posters generally go for $500 to $800; grander four-poster and canopy beds are usually priced between $1,000 and $3,000, depending on the bed's rareness and condition. "Just give us a call," says Mr. Mendes, "or send us a letter telling us your needs, and we will send photos of different beds so you can choose the one you like best." Mendes Antiques is on Route 44 in Rehoboth, Mass. 02769 (seven miles east of Providence, R.I.).

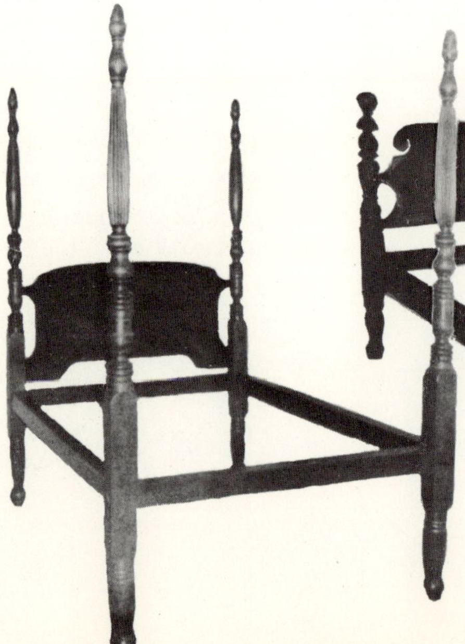

Mario Bellini's Software/Coupé Bed

Mario Bellini, Italy's premier designer of thought-provoking furniture, took some steel and some suede and some heavy-duty zippers and whipped them into the Software/Coupé, one bed that zips into many: a single bed with a headboard (A); a single bed with footboard and headboard (B); a double bed with a full, zipped-together headboard (C), and a double bed with a headboard and a footboard (D). It (or they) is (or are) part of Bellini's Software Collection, which he put together for the Italian furniture company he designs for exclusively: Cassina.

Cassina's, and therefore Mr. Bellini's, furniture is represented exclusively in the United States by Atelier International (595 Madison Avenue, New York, N.Y. 10022), which shows it only to people in "the trade": interior designers, decorators, and architects.

Cassina's multilingual literature on the Software/Coupé describes it this way:

"Model Description: . . . Double beds are composed of two single units ganged together. All units are provided with industrial zipper genging devices for connecting adjacent panels and bolted connectors for joining one unit to another. All units, when produced in fabric or suede, are provided with leather piping on all vertical panel edges, cushions and pillows. This piping is available in special tan and dark brown leathers

A

B

40901

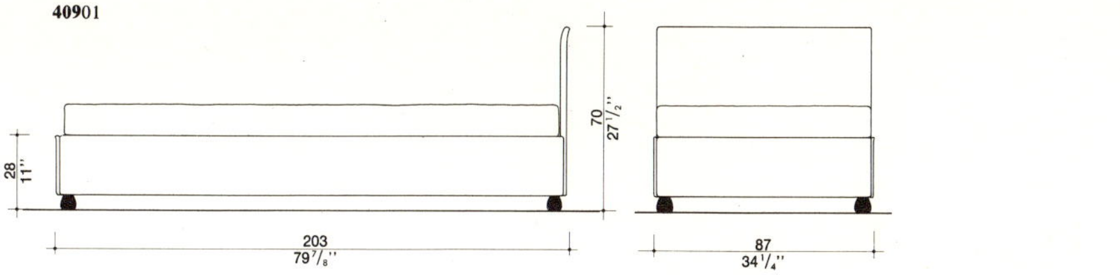

40902

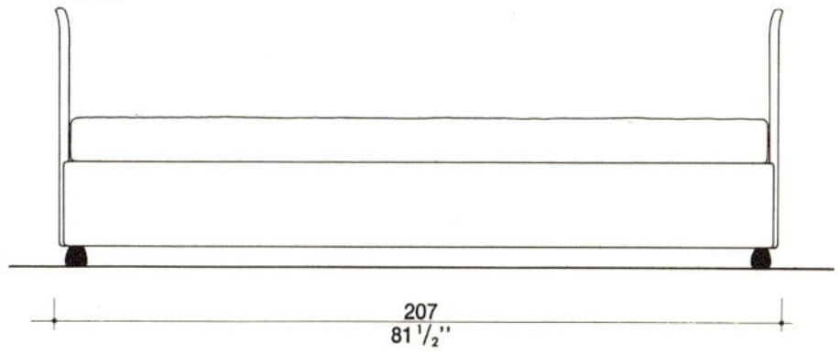

40904

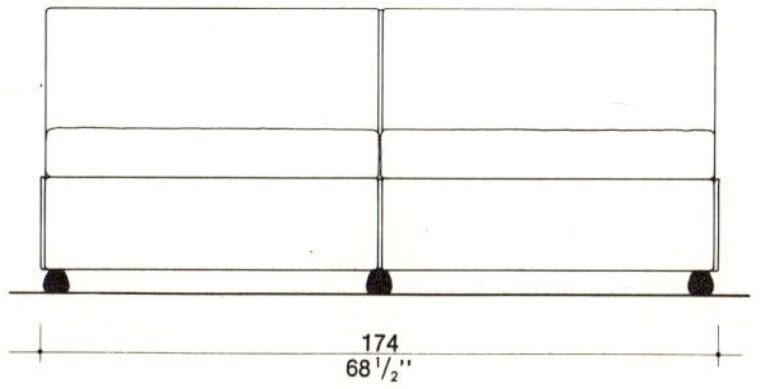

only. Leather upholstery is executed with matching leather piping. All covers are removable.

"Construction: Individually upholstered sub-panels, fabricated from welded steel armatures and spring steel structures cast within a highly sophisticated polyurethane foam, are belted together as required to compose the various seating configurations. Industrial grade zippers are sewn into the panel covers and are employed to gang units together and provide added rigidity. Cushions and pillows are Dacron Fiberfil and/or natural down feather."

Covered in suede, a Software/Coupé with footboard and headboard goes for $2,325, mattress not included.

C

D

An Armchair/Sleeping Bag Called "Idea"

Two Italian designers—one named Baroni, the other Pastori—had a very clever idea; it was so clever, in fact, that they decided to call it "Idea," and what the big idea was, was a little puffy chair that miraculously transforms itself and all its parts into a sleeping bag that doesn't look anything like the chair it was made from. The rigid parts that give the chair its shape come apart and reassemble to make a long rigid base that lifts the sleeping bag off the ground. The sleeping bag itself is the chair's sides, back, and bottom unzipped and folded out into a bed that zips open to be crawled into. And the chair's seat cushion becomes the sleeping bag's pillow.

The Italian manufacturer, Plana/First, adds their description: "An armchair which zips into a convertible sleeping bag bed. Sleeping bag is dry cleanable. All fabric is 100 percent cotton. Structure is of tubular steel with metal springs and foam pads. The sleeping bag is filled with polyester fibers. Chair: 33½ inches by 31½ inches by 29¼ inches high. Bed: 28½ inches by 80¾ inches."

Abitare, 212 East 57th Street, New York, N.Y. 10022, imports the "Idea" armchair/sleeping bag bed and sells it to the public for $495, which isn't really very much to spend for two pieces of furniture.

The "Idea" armchair/sleeping bag bed from Baroni and Pastori: as a puffy little armchair (top), and as a very contemporary sleeping bag (bottom).

The "Idea" armchair/sleeping bag bed, as a partly zipped-open sleeping bag.

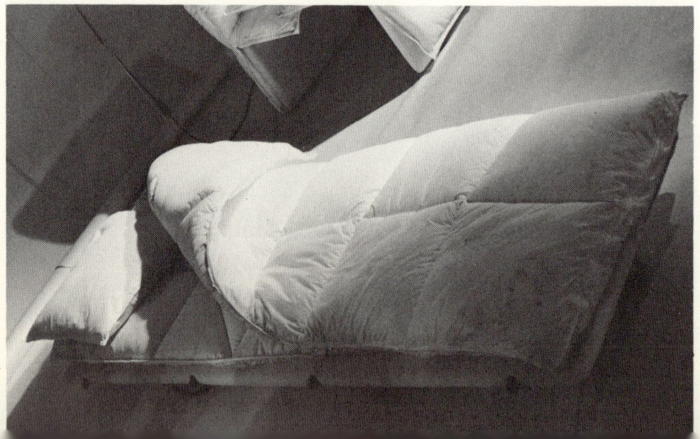

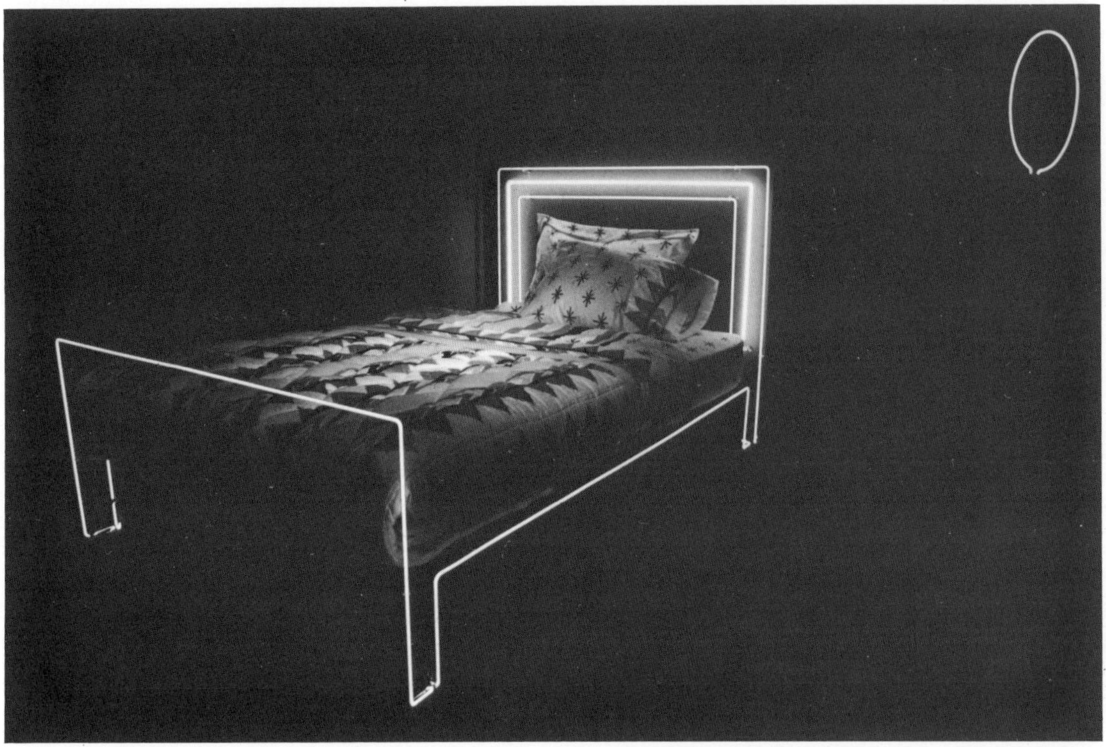

A Neon Bed

The ultimate night light: a neon bed. Wamsutta Mills commissioned it. Let There Be Neon, a gallery of neon art and creator of original neon designs and objects, made it and shares the designing credit with the Wamsutta Display Studio. It's a double bed, and over 50 feet of tubing went into its construction. The center headboard tube contains reddish-orange-glowing neon gas; the remaining tubing contains argon gas, which glows blue. A modified platform bed frame supports the tubing and bedding. Let There Be Neon will design and build a similar one for around $1,500. They are located at 451 West Broadway, New York, N.Y. 10012.

A 1912 Roycroft Bed

Above: *Detail of Roycroft bed headboard, showing the carving that identifies the maker.*

Below: *The Roycroft bed as it appeared in the pages of a 1912 Roycroft catalog. Above and to the right of the bed is the Roycroft orb, the distinctive mark of the Roycrofters that was stamped on many of the items made by the members of the Roycroft community.*

During the closing years of the 19th century and through the greater part of the first two decades of the 20th, a number of individuals and organizations, working within what has come to be called the American Arts and Crafts Movement, were engaged in the production of decorative objects and items of furniture that celebrated, and depended for their manufacture on, the skills of the individual craftsman. The furniture was neo-Gothically spare and angular, constructed from oak and similar wood, and left unpainted in order to display the honesty of the grain. Gustav Stickley was the most important and now most famous maker of such furniture; the most unusual was the Roycroft Shop, part of turn-of-the-century businessman, author, publisher, and Utopian thinker Elbert Hubbard's East Aurora, N.Y., community of printers, artists, and craftsmen. At its peak, over 500 creative individuals lived and worked within the community; they called themselves Roycrofters.

"As stated, these pieces of furniture are strictly hand-made," reads a 1901 advertising circular for Roycroft furniture, "solid oak, severely simple and made to last ninety-nine years, and at the expiration of this time be as good as new. Such work as this has a distinct style that can never be mistaken for something else. We have been making furniture for several years, but it has all been taken as fast as produced, without advertising. . . . No stock of furniture is carried—the pieces are made as ordered, and about two months will be required to fill your order. Every piece is signed by the man who made it."

The circa 1912 Roycroft bed shown here has about thirty years to go before its ninety-ninth birthday, but it's made it this far in A-one condition. And it's become considerably more valuable: Jordan Volpe Gallery (457 West Broadway, New York, N.Y. 10012) owns it and has put a $3,500 price tag on it.

Jordan Volpe also has beds by Gustav Stickley and other important Arts and Crafts furniture makers, in addition to chairs, tables, lamps, art pottery, paintings, and similar items.

Opposite: *Double-size Roycroft bed (circa 1912) on display at Jordan Volpe Gallery.*

Brueton Industries has two names for this bed. Officially, it's the Stainless Steel Radiator Bed by Stanley J. Friedman. In ads for the bed, however, it is labeled, with undisguised pride, the Brueton Bed. It is, according to Brueton's Brueton Bed (or Stainless Steel Radiator Bed) brochure, "a superb marriage of handcrafted stainless steel tubing and custom down tailoring." The bed's frame is made of six 1½-inch-diameter polished stainless steel tubes with a steel platform inner frame mounted on concealed casters. The steel is 304 stainless, the highest grade with the highest possible chrome content. The complete bed includes the mattress, the boxspring, and quilted Brueton sateen fabric and pillows. The king-size bed, with dismantleable frame and a $9,000 price tag, measures 98 inches long by 82 inches wide. The queen ($7,000) is 98 inches long by 64 inches wide; the double ($6,500), 93 by 58 inches; the twin ($5,500), 93 by 43 inches.

Brueton says they sell an average of one Stainless Steel Radiator Bed a day. The identities of the scores of Arabian potentates and American recording stars who've bought them is a closely guarded secret. One Texas millionaire corraled two—covered in black Italian kid leather—at $16,000 apiece. Brueton will also gold plate the frame on request. However, they take such requests and others from interior decorators, designers, and architects only. Brueton's main showroom is at 315 East 62nd Street, New York, N.Y. 10021.

The "Brueton Bed"

A Brass Platform Bed

This queen-size "platform" bed has eight heavy cast-brass "T" joints connecting double brass tube side rails to a matching footboard and headboard. Joao Isabel (see page 52) makes it and sells it for $795.

"Ideal for small apartments, guest rooms and anywhere you'd use a convertible, only better. It's a real full-size platform bed (most convertibles are toy beds) and it's easy to move (ever move a convertible? You should be so strong). By day it's a very comfortable couch. Bedding stores in the base," says Loftcraft's literature describing the ingenuity of their design. The whole thing comes knocked-down in a box along with instructions for putting it together. It takes a full-size mattress and costs $385 in birch, $402 in oak, and $435 in walnut.

For even more information, write Loftcraft, 171 Seventh Avenue, New York, N.Y. 10011.

A Couch/Platform Bed

A Reproduction Gothic Bed

The Gothic Bed no. P300 by Reid Classics combines their post P with headboard no. 300. "This is the best example we have seen in which the design of cluster columns in the ancient Gothic cathedrals is incorporated in furniture for the home," says the Reid Classics catalog. The posts are 89⅝ inches high. The price is $6,720. See page 109.

A close look at two areas of carving on Reid Classics' post P.

A Royal Cow Bed

The bed shown here is both an original and a copy—the original prop bed seen by millions in Cecil B. De Mille's 1956 cast-of-thousands film classic *The Ten Commandments* and a very accurate reproduction of the double-cow-headed couch/bed discovered in the tomb of that well-known 14th-century B.C. Egyptian boy king, Tutankhamen.

The original bed's gilt surface is interrupted by inlays of precious lapis lazuli; the copy's are of blue marble and, like the original's, its horn/sun-disk sections and tails are removable. The 28-inch-high woven sleeping surface is 72 inches long and 35 inches wide, and the overall dimensions are 59 inches high by 86 inches long.

Paramount Pictures, producer of *The Ten Commandments*, spared no expense in producing this bed, sending its maker to Egypt to study the original (in the Cairo Museum) firsthand. Muriel Karasik Gallery (1094 Madison Avenue, New York, N.Y. 10028) is now selling it. If you feel like sparing no expense in acquiring it, it will cost you $23,000.

One of two beds—this one being a famous one-of-a-kind copy of an equally famous original in Cairo—with double cow heads.

An Elephant Bed

A very different species of bed—Bunkus pachydermus?—is this bunk with a trunk (of the proboscidean kind) by Scottish designer Angus Bruce (see page 72). It's all wood with nary a metal or mechanical part, consists of thirty-four separate oil-finished parts (fifteen band-saw-cut birch plywood sections, five ladder rungs, and fourteen dowels), weighs approximately 130 pounds, and comes knocked down and packed flat in a box for $875 (plus freight). Standing up a knocked-down elephant is usually no simple task, but this one easily and quickly and without tools assembles into a beautiful 102-by-60-by-48-inch beast ready to transport young mahouts off on shut-eye safaris and bedtime tiger hunts. Angus Bruce's elephant bunks are born at 398 West Broadway, New York, N.Y. 10012. The time between ordering one and having it shipped is approximately eight weeks. The normal gestation period for an elephant is from nineteen to twenty-one months.

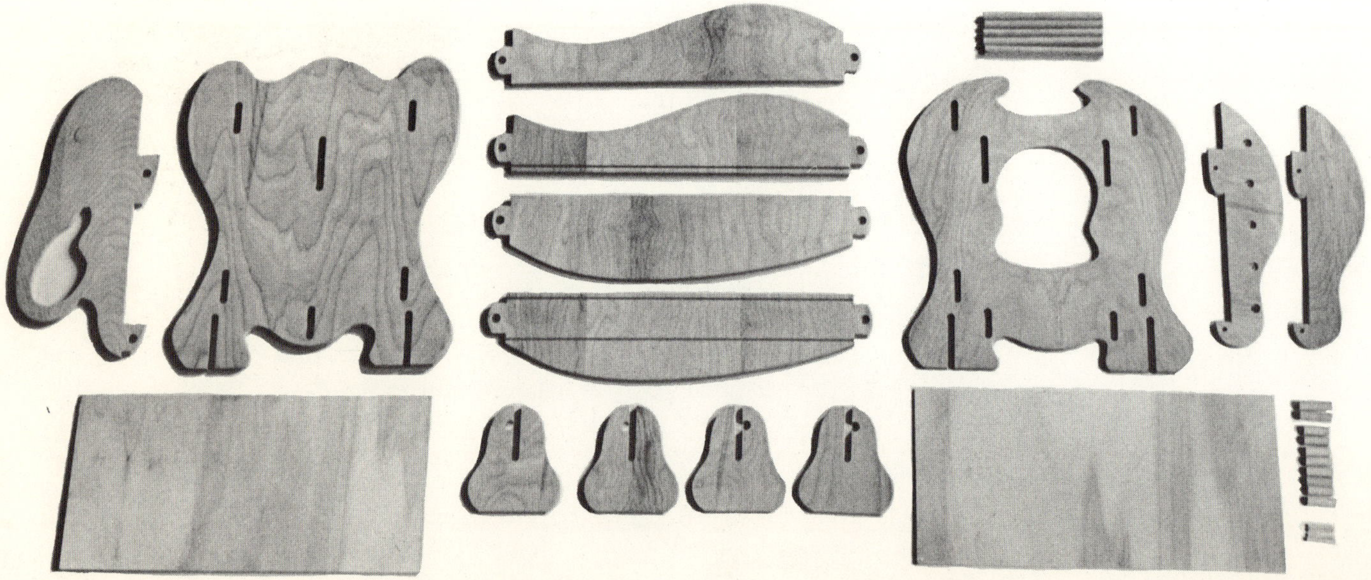

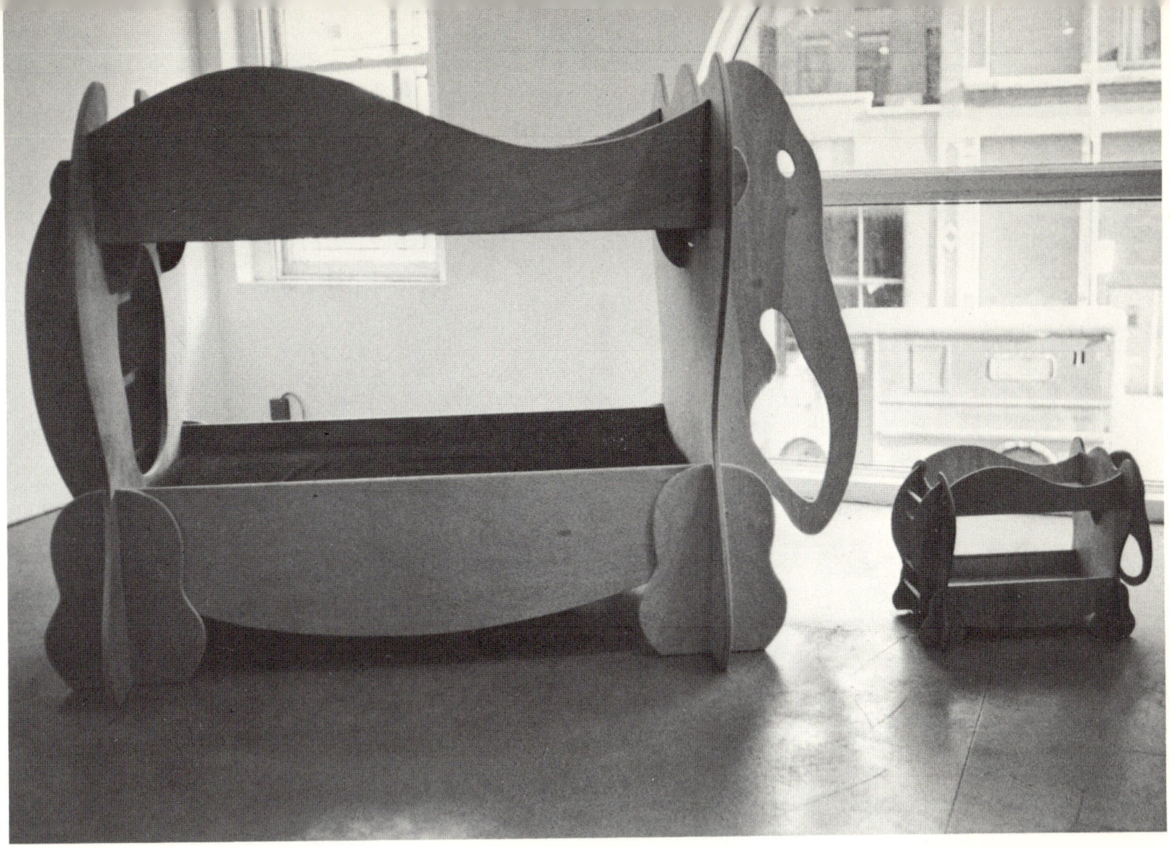

According to the importer, Turner Ltd. (305 East 63rd Street, New York, N.Y. 10021), the "Bonsoir" sleep sofa designed by DeSede of Switzerland "marks a new day in sofa-bed design. Beautifully conceived along flawless horizontal lines, the couch and armchair form a graceful conversation ensemble by day. At night, with just a gentle push and pull, the couch is effortlessly transformed into a double bed."

Available through someone in "the trade" (an interior decorator, designer, or architect) only, the "Bonsoir" sofa is $2,500 in fabric and $3,635 in leather. Closed up, the width is 205 cm (80.7 inches), the depth is 91 cm (35.8 inches), the seat height is 42 cm (16.5 inches), and the overall height is 70 cm (27.5 inches). The open sleeping area is 165 cm (65 inches) by 193 cm (76 inches).

The "Bonsoir" Sleep Sofa

Opposite: *The "Bonsoir" sleep sofa, in its* bonjour *position.*

Right: *The "Bonsoir" saying* "bonsoir."

The "Eletto" Sofa-bed

B&B Italia describes the "Eletto" sofa-bed this way:

"An aluminum and steel frame is imbedded in cold molded polyurethane which is fixed onto steel strip netting. Articulated on various points, it is possible to transform the sofa swiftly into a double bed of exceptional comfort with a simple single rotation.

"Eletto originates from this technical innovation—a sofa which when closed, no one would suspect is a bed—and when opened and it becomes a bed, no one would guess is a sofa. The surface for sleeping is not the same one as for sitting on. Eletto contains an 'instant bed'; sheets, blankets and quilts can be stored in the sofa-bed, and there is even a space for pillows. Should Eletto be placed against a wall, you can open it without having to move it—neither do you have to move its arms, cushions or seats as is usually required to convert a sofa-bed. In addition, there are no visible levers or tie rods on the Eletto, nor do you feel any of the mechanism through the mattress."

The price of an "Eletto" sofa-bed ranges from around $2,000 (C.O.M.—covered in the customer's own material) to a little over $4,000 (covered in the manufacturer's top-grade leather). The mattress—it should measure 61 inches wide, 76 inches long, and 3 inches thick—is not included. Closed, the "Eletto" is 71 inches wide, 43½ inches deep, 29⅝ inches high at the highest point, 24 inches at the arms, and 17 inches at the seat. Opened up, the full depth is 81 inches and the bed height is 15 inches.

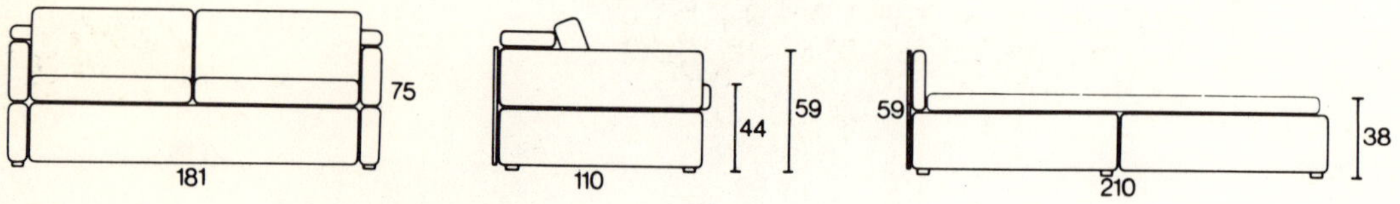

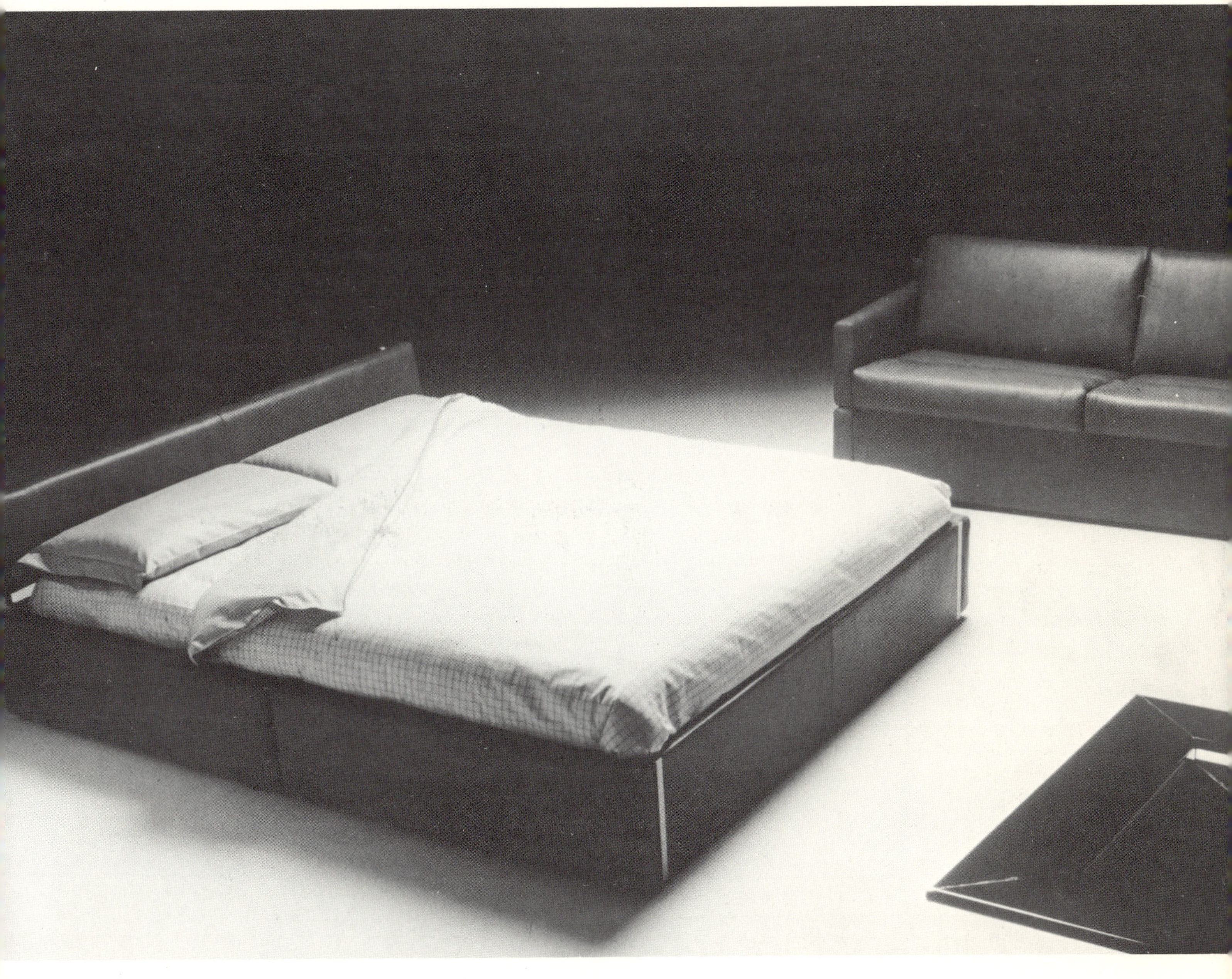

The "Eletto" sofa-bed, designed by Paolo Piva and manufactured in Italy by B&B Italia. B&B America (745 Fifth Avenue, New York, N.Y. 10022) imports and sells it here, but only through architects and interior decorators.

GLOSSARY

Bed Types, Bed Parts, and Things Related to the Bed

AIR BED. A term applied to any inflatable cushion or mattress large enough to support the full body length.

ALCOVE BED. A bed set into a wall recess that is either the same size as the bed or larger. Alcove beds were known in medieval times and became a popular style in France in the middle of the 18th century. Many of the beds found in Pompeii were set into walls and may be the earliest of this type.

ANGEL BED. See *Lit d'ange*.

BALDACHIN. A small canopy shaped like an umbrella and from which curtains were hung.

BALDACHIN BED. A bed set lengthwise against a wall with a baldachin canopy overhead.

BANC LIT. A long seat or bench that can be turned into a bed. Bedding is stored inside when not in use. *Banc lits* were popular in early French Canada and were very similar to American (U.S.) settle beds of the same period. See Settle bed.

BEDBOARD. A rigid board, usually of plywood or a similar material, that is placed under a mattress or between a mattress and boxspring to make the sleeping surface firmer.

BED BOLT. A large bolt that fastens a bed's posts to the side bed rails. Running through the post and into a threaded hole in the end of the rail, it is usually hidden behind a flat plate (normally made of brass) attached to the post by a single screw. The plate slides away to allow access to the bolt. Bed bolt construction is common to most early American four-poster beds.

BED POST. That part of a bed which supports a corner of the bed's framework that carries the mattress and other bedding. Tall posts may carry a canopy and hangings. A bed with short posts is called a lowpost bed. A bed with four tall posts of equal height is called a four-poster.

BED RAILS. The two rails that run along the side of the bed from the foot to the head; these may be attached to a headboard and footboard or to posts at the head and foot. In older beds, ropes strung through holes in the bed rails provided the support for the mattress and bedding.

BED SLATS. Boards laid across a bed's frame on the bed's side rails (or inside its metal frame), upon which the mattress and other bedding are placed. Because of improvements in bedding foundations, bed slats are rapidly becoming a thing of the past.

BEDSPRINGS. Metal springs for chairs and settees were introduced in the middle of the 18th century, and a 19th-century innovation was the mattress-supporting foundation consisting of a wide variety of metal spring arrangements (with the coils running either vertically or horizontally) attached to a rigid frame that was laid on top of the bed's side rails or fitted into the bed's frame. The 20th-century boxspring has almost completely replaced bedsprings.

BEDSTEAD. The name given to the rigid framework of a bed, to distinguish it from the bedding (mattress, boxspring, hangings, etc.).

BOAT BED. See *Lit en bateau.*

BOX BED. A bed entirely enclosed by paneled walls to keep out the cold and separate the bed from the rest of the room. This type of bed first appeared in northern Europe around the 12th century and remained a rural phenomenon into the 20th. An early Canadian version was called a *cabane*. The term is sometimes applied to beds that fold against a wall when not in use.

BOXSPRING. A mattress foundation, developed just before World War II, consisting of a coiled-spring arrangement covered by a thin layer of padding and housed within a cloth-covered wooden frame.

BRASS BED. A bed made entirely or partially of brass, an alloy of copper and zinc. The first brass beds were manufactured in England in the 1830s.

BRIDAL BED. See Marriage bed.

BUNK. A shelflike bed usually attached to a wall and used in places where space is limited, as on a ship.

BUNK BEDS. A pair of narrow (usually twin-size) beds attached one above the other. Patterned after typical Western cowboy bunkhouse beds, they are primarily an item of children's furniture. The upper bunk bed is reached by means of a ladder.

CANOPY. A term used to describe any of various rooflike structures that cover part or all of a bed. A canopy may be suspended from the ceiling, attached to the wall at the head of the bed, be an extension of a tall headboard, or, as is most frequently the case, carried by the posts of the bed.

CANOPY BED. Any bed covered by a canopy.

CAPTAIN'S BED. A type of storage bed consisting of a simple rectangular frame with pull-out drawers beneath a flat surface that accommodates a mattress. It is very popular for children's rooms.

CHAISE LONGUE. See Daybed.

CHIPPENDALE BED. A bed made in the style of English furniture designer Thomas Chippendale (1718–79), a master of the light, feminine Rococo style. The American Chippendale period runs from approximately 1750 to 1785.

CLINOPHOBIA. Fear of beds.

COT. A narrow folding bed consisting of a strong fabric (usually canvas) attached to a collapsible metal or wooden frame.

CRADLE. An infant's first bed, frequently placed on rockers or hung from a framework that allows it to swing.

CRIB. An infant's second bed, having high sides usually composed of thin bars which the baby can hold onto and also look through.

DAYBED. A chair with a slanted back and an extended seat for supporting its occupant's outstretched legs. It is sometimes used as a bed, especially during the day. A more elaborate and plusher type is called a *chaise longue* —or a chaise lounge, but only in America. A French daybed is called a *lit de repos*. The daybed was the forerunner of today's sofa.

DIVAN. A backless sofa of Eastern origin that was frequently placed lengthwise along a wall and occasionally was slept on. The name is also used to denote a bed with no headboard or footboard.

DOME BED. A bed with a canopy shaped like a dome. Beds of this type were most popular in 18-century France.

DUCHESSE BED. A French canopy bed with no posts at the foot, but with a curtained full tester extending from the wall at the head of the bed. The name also refers to an arrangement of two deep chairs or settees facing each other with a cushioned stool connected between. Covered by a single canopy, this piece of furniture was a creation of English furniture designer Thomas Sheraton (1751–1806).

FIELD BED. A relatively light, collapsible bed made of wood or metal and used from the late Middle Ages until the 19th century by travelers who wanted to take their beds with them. Later versions were called tent beds, a term frequently used in connection with light-framed American four-poster beds.

FOOTBOARD. The part of a bed's frame that rises vertically from the foot to a point above the level of the bedding. The footboard was an innovation of the ancient Egyptians, whose beds had footboards but usually lacked headboards.

FOUR-POSTER BED. A bed with four tall posts, one at each corner, usually serving to support a canopy or tester. The four-poster bed as we know it today is a product of the 18th century.

FUTON. A thin stuffed mattress used by the Japanese, usually placed on a straw platform called a *tatami.* It is folded and put away during the day. The sleeper is covered by a thin quilt called a *kakebuton.* The mattress is also called a *shikibuton.*

GOOSENECK BED. A variation of the French Empire-inspired American sleigh bed. This typically symmetrical bed was placed against a wall lengthwise and its front posts only were carved elaborately in the shapes of long-necked geese.

HALF TESTER. See Tester.

HALF-TESTER BED. A bed having a half-tester canopy.

HAMMOCK. A length of canvas, netting, or similar material suspended horizontally between two supports, i.e., two trees, by means of ropes connected to both ends. Used primarily for lounging in modern countries, the hammock is the primary "bed" type in much of the underdeveloped world, especially in parts of South America.

HARVARD FRAME. A metal bed frame with caster-equipped legs into which a boxspring may be set. It adjusts to accept any size boxspring and is designed so that a headboard may be attached.

HIRED MAN'S BED. A simple, sturdy wooden bed with low, sometimes simply turned posts.

HI-RISER. A space-saving invention of the 20th century, a couch with a concealed mattress-in-a-drawer beneath. When pulled all the way out from under the couch, the bottom mattress and frame lift up to the level of the couch cushion and lock into place.

HOLLYWOOD BED. The term used to describe a bed consisting of a headboard, Harvard frame, boxspring, and mattress. A product of the 1940s, the Hollywood-type bed remains the most widely slept on in the United States.

JACKBED. A rustic bed built in frontier cabins during the 18th century. A post was set on the floor, about six feet from one wall and about four feet from another, and timbers were extended from the wall to the post. Slats were placed across the timbers and a straw-filled sack was placed on top.

LIT À LA POLONAISE. An 18th-century French bed having a headboard and a footboard of equal height.

LIT D'ANGE. A bed with a canopy or tester, but with no foot posts. The tester usually covered only part of the bed and was hung with light curtains that were drawn back at the sides next to the head of the bed. Also called an angel bed.

LIT DE REPOS. See Daybed.

LIT EN BATEAU. A bed of the French Empire period that looked like a double-prowed boat.

LOFT BED. A sleeping platform raised to a sufficient height to allow a person to walk under it. A recently popularized, space-saving bed.

LOWPOST BED. A bed with short posts, either simply turned or left plain.

MARRIAGE BED. A term used to refer to the first bed a newly married couple sleeps in. It is also called a bridal bed or nuptial bed. In some cultures in the past, wealthy families had special beds built specifically for the occasion.

MAT. The simplest form of bed, used in many parts of the world to this day. Vegetable fibers—usually woven, plaited, or thatched—are the usual material used.

MATTRESS. The stuffed cushion that is the primary unit of bedding and the part that actually supports and cushions the sleeper. Early mattresses were filled with straw, cotton, animal hair, or feathers. The innerspring mattress wasn't developed until the 1920s. The latest innovation in mattresses is the fluid-filled rubber container used in water beds. A cross between a standard mattress and a water-bed mattress, called a "hybrid," has also been developed.

MURPHY BED. Patented in 1905, the first Murphy In-A-Dor bed was an improvement on the press bed of an earlier era, the spring system for raising and lowering the bed being the major advance.

PALLET. A term used to describe a simple, straw-filled mattress used directly on the floor.

PENCIL-POST BED. An 18th-century American four-poster bed with thin, unadorned posts that gradually taper to almost a point at the top and usually support a light canopy frame.

PILLOW. The cloth case filled with feathers, foam, or similar material that supports and cushions the head during sleep.

PLATFORM BED. A simple shallow box for holding a mattress situated on a slightly smaller pedestal. This bed type originated in Scandinavia in the 1930s and became very popular in the United States in the mid-1970s.

PRESS BED. A bed that folds up into a case that, when closed, resembles a linen closet, or press. A forerunner of the Murphy bed, the press bed was introduced in the 17th century.

QUEEN ANNE BED. A bed from the period named for the reign of Queen Anne (approximately 1707 to 1714 in England and 1720 to 1760 in America). The base of the front posts terminated in the animallike cabriole leg that distinguished furnishings of the Queen Anne period.

RICE BED. A four-poster bed with a rice-stalk pattern carved into the posts. The type was peculiar to the Old South; a plantation owner traditionally passed a rice bed down to his oldest daughter as a wedding gift.

RUSTIC BED. A type of bed made since the 1860s in the Adirondack Mountain region of New York State. The natural shape of the wood used often dictated the design of the bed.

SECRET BED. The name given to early types of convertible beds by their inventors. Secret beds, when not being used as beds, became sofas, bureaus, tables, pianos, and other pieces of furniture.

SETTLE BED. A long benchlike seat with arms and a high back. The seat swings out and down so that the front panels rest on the floor, forming a bed. This type of bed was widely used in Colonial times. A similar bed of the the period was the French Canadian *banc lit*.

SHAKER BED. A very simple bed with an unadorned wooden frame made by the early 19th-century American Quaker sect. It had a rope mattress foundation and either no posts or very low posts. The legs were frequently mounted on wheels so that the bed could be rolled away from the wall during housecleaning.

SHERATON BED. A bed in the style of English furniture designer Thomas Sheraton (1751–1806). Sheraton's furniture was noted for its simplicity, delicacy, and vertical linear grace. One interesting Sheraton design was his so-called summer bed: two beds placed side by side, with a narrow space between them, surmounted by a single canopy. The American Sheraton period dates roughly from 1795 to 1820.

SLEIGH BED. An American version of the French Empire bed. The headboard and footboard, of the same height, were scrolled and looked like sleigh fronts.

SOFA-BED. Any piece of furniture that serves primarily as a sofa and contains a folded-up bedspring/mattress mechanism inside. Also called a couch bed, convertible sofa, or simply a convertible.

SOMNOLOGY. The scientific study of sleep.

SPOOL BED. A common 19th-century American lowpost bed distinguished by its heavily turned posts, both horizontal and vertical.

STUDIO BED. A kind of couch with a bed frame and mattress that slide out from beneath it. Also called a studio couch.

STUMP BED. An early American bed with no posts or footboard, and simple, unadorned legs supporting the frame. The name is sometimes given to beds having no posts to support a tester or canopy. Also called a stump bedstead.

TENT BED. A four-poster bed of relatively modest proportions, having an arched and rounded canopy hung with light curtains. A type of field bed. The terms are sometimes used interchangeably.

TESTER. A flat canopy extending over all or part of a bed. A full tester is usually supported by the bed's posts; a half tester, extending over only the head half of the bed, is frequently supported by a high headboard. Both are sometimes hung from the ceiling.

TESTER BED. Any bed having a tester.

TOURIST BED. A collapsible bed that was attached to the side of an automobile and provided a tentlike shelter. It was invented in the early 20th century.

TRUCKLE BED. A low frame fitted with bedding and designed to fit under a larger bed. A trundle bed had wheels and could be rolled in and out from under the bed; the truckle bed was simply pushed.

TRUNDLE BED. See Truckle bed.

VALANCE. The drapery that hangs around a bedstead, either from the canopy or tester or from the mattress.

WATER BED. A bed having a liquid-filled "puncture-proof" rubber mattress confined in a rigid, heated, waterproof frame. This was an innovation of the early 1970s.

PHOTO CREDITS

Title page left, page 19	Courtesy, The Henry Francis du Pont Winterthur Museum
Title page bottom, pages 41, 47, 95, 119, 137	Courtesy of Sotheby Parke Bernet Inc., New York
Page 5, left	Courtesy of the Pennsylvania Academy of the Fine Arts, Gift of Gaye Cooper, 1973
Page 5, bottom	The Metropolitan Museum of Art, Funds from various donors, 1886
Page 6, top	The Metropolitan Museum of Art
Pages 6 bottom, 7	Photography by Egyptian Exhibition, The Metropolitan Museum of Art
Page 8	The Metropolitan Museum of Art, Gift of J. Pierpont Morgan, 1917
Page 9	The Metropolitan Museum of Art, Rogers Fund, 1905
Page 10	The Metropolitan Museum of Art, Fletcher Fund, 1947: The A. W. Bahr Collection
Page 11	The Metropolitan Museum of Art, Gift of Mrs. Samuel T. Peters, 1926
Page 12	The Metropolitan Museum of Art, Gift of George R. Hann, 1965
Page 13	Courtesy of the Picture Collection, Cooper-Hewitt Museum Library: Smithsonian Institution, New York
Pages 14, 16, 18	Courtesy of the Kubler Collection, Cooper-Hewitt Museum Library: Smithsonian Institution, New York
Page 17, top	Photograph by Jacob A. Riis, Jacob A. Riis Collection, Museum of the City of New York

Page 17, bottom	The Metropolitan Museum of Art, Gift of Paul Martini, 1969
Pages 26, 27	Museum of the City of New York
Page 50	Omnigraphics Inc.
Page 63, top right	Franco Ziglioli
Page 64, bottom	Oberto Gili
Page 75	From "The Bed." Courtesy of the Museum of Contemporary Crafts of the American Crafts Council. Photographer: Ferdinand Boesch
Page 76	Lawrence Cashman
Pages 78, 79	David Nichols
Page 83	Eduardo Nuñez
Page 86, left	Alfredo Anghinelli
Pages 88 top, 154, 155	Turner Ltd.
Page 102	Martin Benjamin
Pages 109 top, 127, 149	Thigpen Photography
Page 130, top	Bill Aller/The New York Times
Pages 140, 141	Aldo Ballo
Page 143	Designer: Let There Be Neon/Wamsutta Display Studio. Photo: Abe Rezny